DUFF GOLDMAN
SUPER GOOD
COOKIES FOR KIDS

HARPER
An Imprint of HarperCollinsPublishers

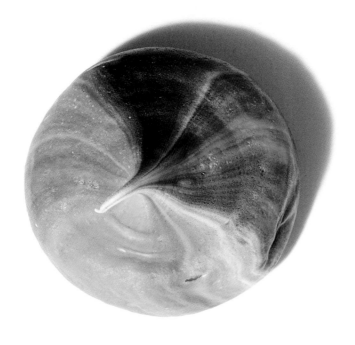

Super Good Cookies for Kids

Copyright © 2022 by Duff Goldman

Photography by Benjamin Turner

Interior design by Laura Palese

Production management by Stonesong

Map art, pp. 66–67 by Shutterstock/Visual Generation

www.harpercollinschildrens.com

Library of Congress Control Number: 2022933410

ISBN 978-0-06-325423-7

22 23 24 25 26 PC/TC 10 9 8 7 6 5 4 3 2 1

First Edition

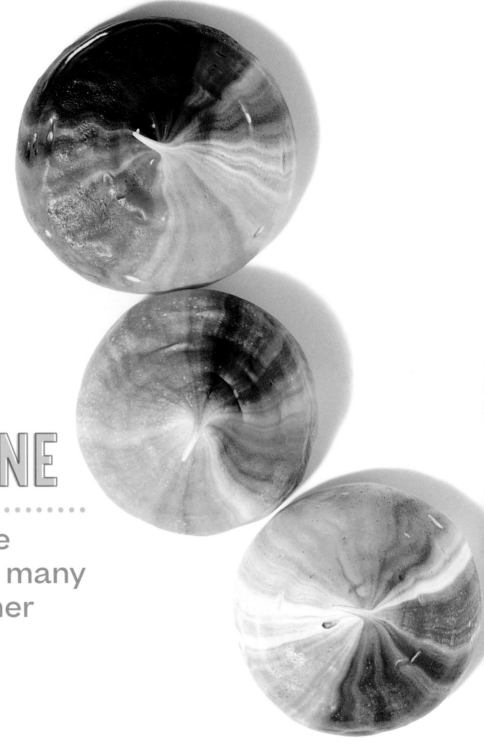

FOR
JOSEPHINE

You and me are
gonna bake so many
cookies together

Contents

MY COOKIE PHILOSOPHY 8 • KITCHEN SAFETY 10 • KITCHEN BASICS 12
EQUIPMENT 14 • INGREDIENTS 20 • BEFORE YOU START 25

CHAPTER 1
Thin Cookies
26

CHAPTER 2
Thick Cookies
38

CHAPTER 3
Mound Cookies
52

CHAPTER 4
International Cookies
64

CHAPTER 5
Sandwich Cookies
88

CHAPTER 6
Unclassifiable Cookies
104

CHAPTER 7
Decorated Cookies
122

CHAPTER 8
Things with Cookies in Them
136

CHAPTER 9
Things That Are Sorta Cookies
146

CHAPTER 10
Holiday Cookies
162

CHAPTER 11
Gluten-Free Cookies
184

CHAPTER 12
Macarons
196

GLOSSARY 204 • MEASUREMENT CONVERSIONS 205 • INDEX 206
ACKNOWLEDGMENTS 208

MY COOKIE
PHILOSOPHY

When I was just a little Duff, one of my warmest and happiest preschool memories was having milk and cookies and then taking a nap. That actually sounds wonderful. I'm going to go have milk and cookies and take a nap right now.

Okay, I'm back. Much better. Where were we? Oh yeah—cookies. There are a lot of aspects about cookies. I love that there are so many different kinds of cookies. Every culture around the world has some kind of cookie, and you can learn a lot about people by the different foods they eat. One of my favorite things to do when I travel is to go to grocery stores. Seeing the kinds of things people like to snack on can really help you understand who they are.

Another thing I enjoy about cookies is that you can get a recipe and bake some cookies, and the very first time you try, you can actually make something really delicious. And then . . . you can spend the rest of your life getting better at making them. Making a good cookie isn't hard. Making an *amazing* cookie . . . that takes practice. You have to develop a relationship with your oven so you know how long to bake your cookies. You have to figure out just how thick to slice the cookies or how much batter to drop onto the sheet pan. You learn which kinds of cookies are better when you bake them as soon as you mix them, and which are best after you put them in the freezer for a few minutes before they hit the oven. Sometimes you want a fat, chewy cookie. Sometimes you want a thin, crispy cookie. Wanna know how to make both? Read on, O child.

I could go on and on about why cookies are so awesome, but I think the thing I love the most about cookies is that they are meant to be shared. You never bake just two cookies. You always bake a whole bunch. And when you give a cookie that you baked to someone who needs a cookie—and we all need a cookie now and then—it makes you glow inside when you see their face light up. Cookies are blessings. They're little hugs that you can give to someone. Nothing says "I love you" like a warm cookie.

KITCHEN SAFETY

Baking is fun. Getting hurt is not fun. Let's bake some cookies and be safe while we do it. Here are some tips on how to make awesome cookies without the pain.

Keep the kitchen clean: Clean the kitchen before you start baking so there is nothing in your way. Clean the kitchen as you go so things don't pile up. Clean the kitchen when you are done so everything goes back where it is supposed to be.

Know what is dangerous: Kitchens are full of shiny and interesting tools, and some of them can be very dangerous. Go through the kitchen with an adult and make sure you know everything you need them to help you with—like knives, the oven, and the stove.

Wash your knives by hand and never, ever leave them in the sink: Don't hide something sharp in the sink. Someone else might not know it is there. Knives also get dull in the dishwasher, and dull knives are dangerous knives. With an adult's supervision, always wash them carefully by hand and dry them before putting them back where they go.

Keep chemicals and food separate: Kitchens contain chemicals, usually for cleaning, that should never be near food. Keep the cleaning chemicals like soap and bleach under the sink and never store food in the same cabinet.

Things get hot: When you are baking, sometimes there can be multiple hot pans in the kitchen. If you've taken a hot pan off the stove, place a clean towel over it so everyone can see that it is not to be touched until it cools off. Don't put hot things on wood or plastic. Set them on the stovetop or a cooling rack or a trivet.

Don't slip: Baking usually involves oil, butter, or other fatty, slippery things. If you make a mess on the floor, stop what you are doing and clean it up immediately so nobody slips on it. Also, fat is flammable, so if you spill oil or butter on the stove or in the oven, turn everything off, let it cool down, and then clean it up before continuing.

Don't try to do too much by yourself: Cooking with friends and family is fun, and sometimes you need a hand carrying something that is heavy or holding things steady when you only have two hands. No flyin' solo. Use the buddy system and have an adult present.

Fires can happen in the kitchen: Make sure you know where the fire extinguisher is and how to use it. And never pour water on a kitchen fire—kitchen fires are usually grease related and water can make them burn hotter and faster. If a fire breaks out and you cannot find the fire extinguisher, use flour to smother it. And if there is a fire, yell for help. Make sure the adults know there is a fire so they can help you deal with it safely.

Keep the oven clean: If you bake something and it drips into the oven, make sure you wait until the oven cools off and then clean it up. Oven drippings will smoke (which will set off the fire alarm) and can catch fire.

Kitchen tools aren't toys: I know they are cool to look at and fun to use, but kitchen tools are tools. They are sharp, powerful, and hot and can seriously hurt you. Respect your kitchen and its tools.

Water and electricity don't mix: Keep the radio, phones, tablets, and computers away from wet things. Electric shocks are awful. I like listening to music in the kitchen, so I keep my radio high up and away from everything I'm working with.

Keep the food safe: Clean your tools and counters with soap and water and disinfect with distilled white vinegar. Use your nose—if an ingredient doesn't smell right, don't use it. And remember the number one rule: if you wouldn't eat it, don't serve it to anyone else.

Adult supervision: THIS IS IMPORTANT.
Any time you're working in the kitchen, always make sure you have an adult present. They'll help keep accidents from happening and help keep you from you getting hurt—and they're also great for reaching things on higher shelves!

KITCHEN BASICS

The kitchen is my favorite room in the house. We cook here, we eat here, we talk here. It's my laboratory. It's my office. It's a special place. Get to know your kitchen and all the tools and gadgets and foods that are in it. Find out what different tools do and try using them in a recipe. Smell the different spices and see if there's something you want to add to your next cookie. Let your imagination run wild and see what you come up with—maybe you'll invent the next big thing. Here are a few tips to get you started.

Cracking eggs: Always crack eggs on a flat surface instead of on the side of a bowl. They shatter less this way and you won't get shells in your cookie dough.

Separating eggs: When you separate eggs, you have to make sure you don't get any of the yellow into the white. Egg whites won't whip up if there is any yolk in them. Crack the egg in half and pass the yolk back and forth in the eggshell, letting the white drop into a bowl below.

Preheating the oven: When you are baking cookies, you usually have to put the cookies in the oven as soon as you mix them, so it is important that the oven is ready when the cookies are ready. Usually about twenty minutes or so before you think you will be baking, turn the oven on and get it hot so you don't have to wait later on.

Cooling stuff: You gotta cool cookies fast, because if they stay on a hot sheet pan, they'll keep baking and may overbake. The best way to cool cookies fast is on a wire rack. This gets the cookies off the hot pan and allows air to circulate all the way around them so they cool faster.

Room-temperature ingredients: Most recipes will specify what temperature the butter should be. For most cookies, the butter should be at room temperature. If I know I'm baking tomorrow, I look at my recipe and see what temperature my butter should be. If it needs to be room temperature, I set it out on the counter the night before and then my butter is ready when I am. I also like baking with room-temperature eggs because they mix into recipes much easier than cold ones, and warm egg whites make fluffier meringue.

Using a stand mixer: Make sure that the bowl is clean before you start adding ingredients. Also, make sure you have the right attachment for the job. Some doughs are heavier than others and require the paddle or even the dough hook, while lighter doughs and batters call for the whisk attachment. Stand mixers are very powerful, so you don't ever want to stick anything in them while they are working. This includes spatulas and fingers. Also, don't turn the mixer on too high too fast. If there are loose ingredients like flour in the bowl and you turn the mixer on high, you'll be cleaning the kitchen for the rest of the day.

Making a double boiler: To make a double boiler for melting chocolate and a few other things, put a small amount of water in a pot. Get a metal bowl that is a little larger than the pot and place that on top of the pot. Make sure that the bottom of the bowl doesn't touch the water and that the flame under the pot is low enough that it doesn't reach around the sides of the pot and heat the edges of the bowl. All you need is the water at a simmer, so keep the heat down. Put your chocolate (or butter, or whatever else you're melting) in the bowl, and the steam rising underneath will melt it gently.

Creaming butter and sugar: This step is in almost all the recipes in this book. This is when you put room-temperature butter and sugar in the bowl and mix until light and fluffy. This ensures that your ingredients will mix in easy and gives you a base to build the rest of the dough on. Make sure to scrape down the bowl a few times so you know the butter and sugar are mixed evenly.

Folding: Folding happens when you have to mix two or more ingredients gently. Usually if you are folding meringue or whipped cream into something, you want to be gentle so all the air you whipped into your stuff doesn't get knocked out. To fold, use a rubber spatula and gently mix the ingredients by lifting up the batter from one side and folding it over the other.

Toasting nuts: Always toast your nuts! Turn the oven on to 325°F and put the nuts on a dry pan. Toast them in the oven for a few minutes, or until you can smell the delicious nuttiness. Let them cool before using.

EQUIPMENT

Here's a list of most of the tools and equipment you'll need to successfully bake cookies. Don't worry if you don't have everything on this list. Where there's a will, there's a way! If there is an alternative to the more obscure things on this list, I'll let you know. If you have an oven, a bowl, and something flat and metal, you can bake cookies. Everything else is just gravy.

Sheet pans: Flat, heavy-gauge aluminum sheet pans work best. Thin, cheap cookie sheets twist and warp in the oven and make your cookies bake weird. If you are buying professional-grade sheet pans, you want the half-sheet size. Full-size sheet pans don't fit in most home ovens. And let me repeat: *cheap cookie sheets are garbage*. They will always frustrate you and let you down. Get two quality sheet pans and leave the cheapo cookie sheets in the kitchenware aisle of the grocery store.

Parchment paper: You can buy parchment paper precut into sheets that fit perfectly on most sheet pans; get the half-sheet size to fit your pans. Parchment paper is also good for making funnels for dry ingredients and for making tiny paper piping bags.

Wire rack: Cookies need to be transferred to a wire rack after baking so they cool as fast as possible and don't steam and get soggy on the bottom. All my wire racks fit exactly into my sheet pans, so I don't drip or drop crumbs all over the counter. If you don't have a wire rack, you might have an extra rack in your oven. Pull it out, set it on the counter, and use that.

Rolling pin: I like a straight rolling pin. Not tapered and no handles, old-school.

Rolling pin guide: Rolling pin guides are heavy-duty flexible latex strips that you put on the table or counter to roll a dough to a specific thickness. It's important to have your dough at a uniform thickness so the cookies bake evenly.

Cookie scoops: These are often sold in sets of three: 1 tablespoon, 2 tablespoons, and 3 tablespoons—or small, medium, and large.

Piping bags: I like the big disposable plastic piping bags. You can get reusable piping bags, but clean them once and see if you still like them after. If you don't have piping bags, you can use a quart- or gallon-size plastic baggie.

Cookie extruder: Cookie extruders (also called cookie presses) are usually used for making spritz cookies. You put the dough in the canister of the extruder, then press it out through a die (a metal disc with a cut-out pattern) onto your sheet pan. They have lots of different dies that make cookies in fun shapes.

Cookie molds: There are many different cookie molds you can get for all different kinds of cookies. There are special pans for shortbread, and wooden molds for mooncakes, ma'amoul cookies, and pfeffernuesse. Some of the filled cookies, like mooncakes and ma'amoul, can also be baked in a mini-muffin pan. They won't have the fancy embossed pattern, but they'll still be delicious.

Cookie cutters: There are literally millions of different kinds of cookie cutters. Every serious baker has a collection of their favorite cookie cutters. Mine is a buffalo. If you don't have any cookie cutters, you can freeze your cookie dough and then, with adult supervision, cut shapes out with a paring knife or X-Acto knife. Or if you're like me and love the hardware store, you can get some aluminum flashing and create your own cookie cutter shapes!

Stand mixer: These are not cheap, but if you are going to try to bake more than twice a year, I highly recommend you ask your parents to get one (if they don't have one already). If they don't wanna spend that kinda dough (ha ha), they can probably find a good hand mixer for a lot less money. The nice thing about hand mixers is that you don't have to scrape the bowl as much.

Food processor: Food processors are not cheap, but when you use one, it's hard not to think, "How does anyone bake without one of these?" Lots of cookie recipes in this book rely on a food processor to mix the dough.

Waffle iron: Some cookies, namely stroopwafels and ice cream cones, are baked in a special thin waffle iron. My waffle iron is electric and plugs into the wall, but there are also waffle irons that go directly on the stove. They take some getting used to, but they are usually less expensive.

Kitchen scale: Measuring cups and spoons are good, but when you weigh your ingredients, you save LOTS of time and your recipes are much more accurate.

Refrigerator/freezer: When you're baking cookies, make sure you clean off a shelf so you have a free flat space that's big enough to fit a sheet pan.

Oven thermometer: Cookies have to bake at specific temperatures, and just setting your oven to 350°F doesn't mean it's actually exactly 350°F in there—some ovens run hotter, some run cooler. An oven thermometer is a little thermometer that hangs inside the oven and tells you what temperature it really is.

Sifter: Get in the habit of always sifting flour and powdered sugar. Some of these recipes call for it specifically. You can use a round mesh strainer, or a pointy cone-shaped one, or a fancy flat one called a tamis (pronounced "tammy"). I use a tamis . . . just sayin'.

Rubber spatulas: Scrape! You have to scrape the bowl when you are mixing wet and dry stuff together. Scrape! Often!

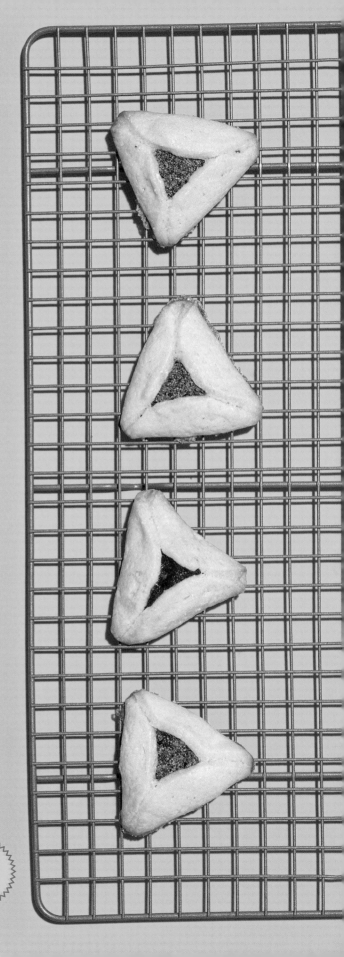

Wire rack

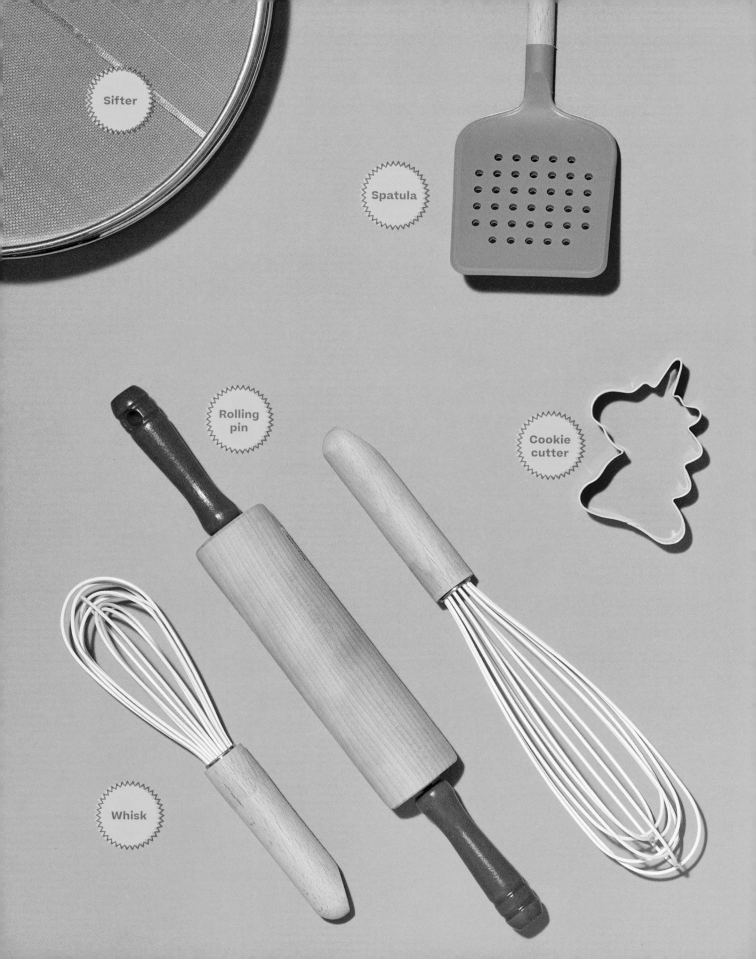

Sifter

Spatula

Rolling pin

Cookie cutter

Whisk

Piping
tips

Mixing
bowls

Piping
bags

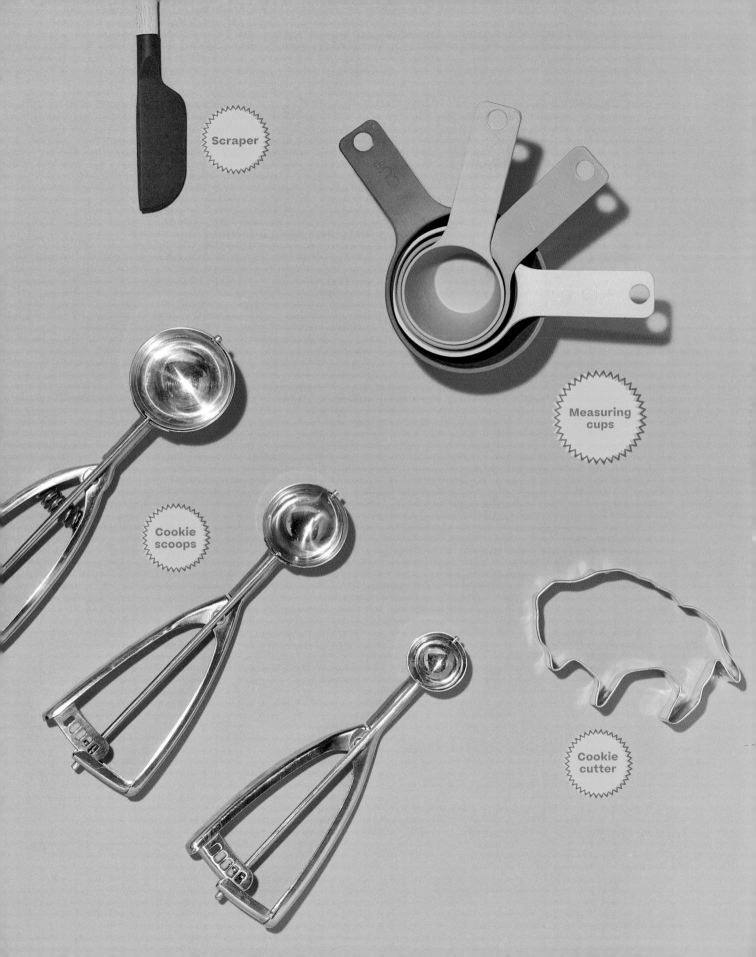

Scraper

Measuring cups

Cookie scoops

Cookie cutter

INGREDIENTS

Most cookie recipes use roughly the same ingredients with a few variations or additions here and there. The difference is the amount of each ingredient used and how those ingredients are incorporated into the recipe. Here's a quick guide to some of the more common ingredients we'll be using for our cookies.

Flour: There are loads of different kinds of flour out there. Usually when you see the word "flour" by itself, it is referring to flour made from wheat. Wheat flour is made by grinding up wheat kernels. By using different species of wheat, flour millers can control what type of wheat flour they produce. Some flour has more protein and less starch, which makes it good for things like bagels and pizza dough. Other kinds of flour have less protein and more starch, good for things like cakes and pastries. And then there's flour that is right in the middle, which is great for muffins (and cookies!). Flour with lots of protein is called "bread flour" and flour with the least amount of protein is "cake flour." The flour right in the middle is called "all-purpose flour." There's also whole wheat flour, which is different from white flour in that the bran of the wheat kernel is also ground up instead of being sifted out. This flour is also called "graham flour" and it's the flour we'll use for graham crackers.

There are lots of other kinds of flours that are made by grinding up all kinds of things. Almond flour is made up of ground almonds. Oat flour is made up of ground oats. There's flour made from teff, amaranth, and corn. There's even flour made from ground-up crickets! (If you made flour from sunflower seeds, would it be called "sunflower flour"?)

Butter: Most cookie recipes need some kind of fat. If there wasn't any fat, these recipes would just make weird-tasting crackers. Butter is the best fat for most of the cookies in this book. It does its job by making the cookies tender and moist, but it also tastes really good. Vegetable shortening would work, but only butter tastes like butter. Some of these recipes call for brown butter. Contrary to popular belief, brown butter does not come from brown cows. It is butter that is melted in a pan and cooked until all the water boils out, so the butter caramelizes and smells amazing. Brown butter also makes cookies sandier in texture because all the water is gone. It doesn't make the flour mushy. For the recipes in this book that call for brown butter, you can use not-brown butter, but you will then have, in my opinion, an inferior cookie.

Eggs: When chefs talk about eggs, usually we are talking about eggs from chickens. I have cooked with all kinds of eggs: quail eggs, goose eggs, duck eggs, even ostrich eggs! Most baking recipes use chicken eggs as the standard. To be more specific, large chicken eggs. Supermarkets also sell medium eggs and extra-large eggs, but large eggs are the standard for baking. A large egg is 1½ ounces. The egg white is 1 ounce, and the yolk is ½ ounce. So if you don't have large eggs but you have medium ones or jumbo ones, just do the math and figure out how much the eggs in your recipe weigh, then measure out that amount from the eggs you have. Brown butter does not come from brown cows, but brown eggs do come from brown chickens. There is absolutely zero difference between the insides of brown and white eggs. Zero. Zilch. Nada. None. There is a difference between chickens that are only fed corn and chickens that also get protein in their diet. When you crack an egg and the yolk is pale and light yellow, that chicken only ate grains. When you crack an egg and the yolk is a deep orange color, that chicken got lots of grubs and bugs. The darker the yolk, the happier the chicken, the better the egg tastes.

Vanilla extract

GRADE AA
BUTTER
NET WT. 4 OZ. (113 grams)

Cinnamon

Sugar: Cookies need a little something sweet. Most of the time, we'll use granulated sugar. Granulated sugar comes from sugarcane and sugar beets. They crush the sugarcane and sugar beets, extract the juice, boil it down, and purify it. This makes granulated white sugar and also molasses. Molasses is used in several of the recipes in this book. It makes cookies taste richer and makes them moist. Brown sugar is granulated sugar that has some molasses added to it. Some of the sweetness in a cookie recipe can also come from corn syrup, which is a liquid sugar made from corn. Honey is another source of sweetness, but you have to be careful with it—it can make cookies too wet, and then they bake weird. Honey is also much, much sweeter than granulated sugar. If you want to use honey in a recipe, it's best to use just a small amount and not replace all the white sugar in direct proportion.

Brown sugar

FUN FACT: butterscotch is caramel made from brown sugar.

Eggs

Spices: Spices, things like cinnamon and nutmeg, are what give cookies their personality. Some cookies have cloves, ginger, or allspice. Some cookies even have pepper! I like Christmas for lots of reasons, but one of them is because of all the cookies. And nothing says "Christmas cookies" to me like all the spices in them. I also love smelling the different spices and imagining where they came from. Spices come from all over the world, and sometimes when I smell a spice, I can imagine what it is like where that spice came from. Try it.

Vanilla: Vanilla is made from a special orchid. It grows on vines in hot, humid places and is really difficult to grow. That's what makes vanilla so special. It's used in lots of recipes and gives baked things a distinct flavor. Vanilla also makes chocolate taste more chocolaty. Most of the vanilla that goes in recipes is in the form of vanilla extract, where the flavor of the vanilla bean is extracted into a liquid. Sometimes you can find actual vanilla beans, and you can cut them open and use the seeds for flavor. When you open the vanilla bean, the scent is like nothing you have ever smelled before. It is really special. When you are buying vanilla extract, make sure you are buying pure vanilla extract that is made from actual vanilla beans. There is also "imitation" vanilla extract. Imitation vanilla is made from wood pulp left over from the papermaking process and tastes very artificial. It is good for some things, like cream filling in sandwich cookies or bright white buttercream on cakes, but for cookies, get the real stuff.

Chocolate: Chocolate is made from cocoa pods, which are the fruit of the cocoa tree. The pulp is harvested and dried in the sun, then processed and separated into cocoa butter and cocoa powder. The butter is just the fat from the pod. The powder is the dried fiber of the pod. Cocoa powder is used by itself in all kinds of chocolate cookies and brownies where you want a rich chocolate flavor. Cocoa powder and cocoa butter are also mixed back together to create chocolate. Dark chocolate is a mixture of cocoa powder, cocoa butter, and sugar. Milk chocolate is cocoa powder, cocoa butter, sugar, and milk. White chocolate is cocoa butter, sugar, and milk, but no cocoa powder. Chocolate chips are usually dark chocolate, but there are all kinds, even butterscotch and peanut butter!

Marshmallows

All-purpose
flour

Granulated
sugar

Chocolate

Molasses

BEFORE YOU START

Read your recipe: Make sure you have everything you need before you start baking. You don't want to have to go to the store in the middle of mixing some cookie dough. Also, you want to know what lies ahead so you can be prepared for every step.

Organize your space: Make sure the oven is clean, all your equipment is where it should be, and there is space in the fridge and/or freezer if you need it.

Take notes: My recipes work for me, but you might want to change some stuff. That's good, that's how recipes happen. Take a pen and write down notes. Draw pictures. Leave yourself clues as to how you can make any recipe better next time you make it.

Always make extra: Do you need twenty cookies? Make thirty. They won't go to waste. Sometimes it's good to be the one with fresh cookies. I've made lots of friends that way.

Follow the directions: In baking, there is some real science going on, like chemistry and physics. If you don't measure correctly and don't do things in the proper order, whatever you are making will probably not be as good as it could be.

CHAPTER 1

THIN COOKIES

LET'S START WITH THIN COOKIES. These are probably my favorite kind of cookies. Some thin cookies are crispy. Some are chewy and more like candy. Thin cookies are basically butter and sugar held together with *juuuuust* enough flour. These cookies are more delicate and harder to move around, package, and sell in a store, which is why most cookies we see at the grocery store are either super dry and stable or really dense and thick. Thin, crispy cookies, the best ones, really only exist at home and even then, only for a short while. They're rare and, therefore, wonderful.

MAKES 30 COOKIES

TUILES

INGREDIENTS

¾ cup (150 grams)	**granulated sugar**
½ cup (1 stick/113 grams)	**butter**, at room temperature
3	**egg whites**
1 teaspoon	**pure vanilla extract**
Pinch of	**kosher salt**
½ cup (60 grams)	**all-purpose flour**

Tuiles are really cool to make. You cut out a stencil from a coffee can lid or other thin piece of plastic, then use that stencil to create a cookie with a very specific shape. These cookies are fantastic decorations for cakes and pies and desserts. You can airbrush them and pipe chocolate on them, too, and make them into anything you want. While they are still hot, you can even shape them into spirals and tubes.

1 In a medium bowl, gently mix the sugar and the butter until combined. It doesn't have to be super smooth at this point. Add the egg whites one at a time and mix until they are incorporated. Now add the vanilla and the salt and give it a good mix. Finally, add the flour. Gently stir until the batter comes together and looks smooth. Refrigerate for 2 to 3 hours.

2 While the batter is in the fridge, cut out stencils from a coffee can lid or a deli container lid. Preheat the oven to 350°F.

3 On a flat surface, line a sheet pan with parchment paper. Place your stencils on the parchment and apply a thin layer of the batter. Lift the stencil to reveal the shape! Repeat until you run out of room on the pan. Bake for 8 to 10 minutes, until the cookies are golden brown on the edges and lighter brown in the middle.

4 If you are shaping the cookies, you have to do it right when they come out of the oven, while they're still warm. You only have a few seconds! If the cookies are supposed to be flat, immediately remove the parchment from your busted, dented, warped cookie sheet and set it on a flat surface so the cookies cool super flat.

MAKES 25 COOKIES

LACE
• COOKIES •

Lace cookies are really special. They are super delicate and you can only really get the best ones by making them at home. They're too fragile to package and sell in stores. They are the absolute perfect mix of sugar, butter, and flour. Just enough flour to barely hold together a bunch of delicious caramelized butter and sugar.

INGREDIENTS

½ cup (65 grams)	**blanched almonds**
2 tablespoons (28 grams)	**butter**, at room temperature
¼ cup (50 grams)	**granulated sugar**
¼ cup (54 grams)	lightly packed **light brown sugar**
¼ cup (82 grams)	**light corn syrup**
Pinch of	**kosher salt**
¼ cup (30 grams)	**all-purpose flour**

1 Preheat the oven to 375°F. Line a few sheet pans with parchment paper.

2 With a knife, carefully chop the almonds so you get gravel-size pieces. Spread them over a sheet pan and toast them in the oven for 6 minutes. Carefully remove them from the oven and let them cool before using.

3 In a small pot, combine the butter, both sugars, the corn syrup, and the salt and heat over medium-low heat, stirring to melt the butter and sugar. When the mixture is smooth, remove it from the heat and stir in the flour and toasted almonds.

4 Scoop 2 tablespoons of the batter onto the prepared pans for each cookie. Make sure you leave room for the cookies to spread. I usually bake 2 or 3 cookies per pan, depending on how big I want them.

5 Bake for 5 to 8 minutes, or until the edges are golden brown and the middles are still a bit pale (they will continue to bake on the pan as they cool). Remove from the oven and cool on the pan for 5 to 6 minutes, then move the cookies to a wire rack to cool completely.

MAKES A LOT OF COOKIES

Moravian SPICE

• COOKIES •

These cookies come from the northeastern part of the United States. Members of the Moravian Church built elaborate Nativity scenes during Christmas and invited people to come and see them and have cookies. Sometimes the best part of cookies is making friends and sharing them. *Don't freak out*—but there's mustard in these cookies. Just try them before you say you don't like them. I promise they're delicious.

1 In the bowl of a stand mixer fitted with the paddle attachment, cream together the butter and brown sugar. Scrape the bowl and add the molasses and egg yolk. Beat on high speed until smooth.

2 In another bowl, whisk together the flour, salt, baking powder, baking soda, cinnamon, ginger, cloves, nutmeg, cardamom, white pepper, and mustard powder. Turn the mixer on low and add the flour mixture to the butter mixture a spoonful at a time. Pause while mixing to scrape the bowl a few times so everything gets combined.

3 Place a piece of parchment paper on the counter and shape a small lump of dough into a rectangle on top. Place another piece of parchment on top. Roll the dough out until it's *super thin*! Like a sixteenth of an inch thick. Leave the dough between the parchment and repeat with the rest of the dough, stacking the dough and parchment on a sheet pan as you go. Freeze the dough for 30 minutes.

4 Preheat the oven to 325°F. Line a few sheet pans with parchment.

5 Remove one sheet of dough from the freezer at a time and cut cookies. Use animal-shaped cookie cutters because that's traditional (Nativity scenes have lots of animals). Place the cut cookies on the prepared sheet pans and freeze for 15 more minutes.

6 Take the cookies out of the freezer and sprinkle with cinnamon sugar. Bake for 10 minutes, rotating the pan after 5 minutes so the cookies bake evenly. Remove from the oven and let cool before eating.

INGREDIENTS

6 tablespoons (¾ stick/85 grams)	**butter**, at room temperature
¾ cup (150 grams)	lightly packed **light brown sugar**
¼ cup (70 grams)	**blackstrap molasses**
1	**egg yolk**
1⅔ cups (200 grams)	**all-purpose flour**
Big pinch of	**kosher salt**
½ teaspoon	**baking powder**
½ teaspoon	**baking soda**
1 teaspoon	**ground cinnamon**
Pinch of	**ground ginger**
Pinch of	**ground cloves**
Pinch of	**ground nutmeg**
Pinch of	**ground cardamom**
Pinch of	**ground white pepper**
Pinch of	**mustard powder**
	cinnamon sugar, for dusting

MAKES 24 COOKIES

Duff's Killer
PECAN
· COOKIES ·

INGREDIENTS

1 cup (2 sticks/226 grams)	**butter**, at room temperature
¾ cup (160 grams)	lightly packed **dark brown sugar**
1	**egg yolk**
Pinch of	**kosher salt**
1 cup (139 grams)	**all-purpose flour**
⅔ cup (73 grams)	chopped **pecans**, lightly toasted
24	**pecan halves** (optional)

I don't know why I have this recipe. I was digging through my recipe books and found it, and in big underlined words it says "THESE ARE GREAT." I think you'll agree. They're thin and kinda chewy like candy, but also nutty and golden brown. Seriously, these are great.

1 In a large bowl, cream the butter, brown sugar, egg yolk, and salt using a stand or hand mixer. Add the flour and toasted pecan pieces and fold them in by hand. Leave the dough in the bowl and refrigerate for 30 to 45 minutes.

2 Preheat the oven to 325°F. Line two sheet pans with parchment paper.

3 Place tablespoon-size scoops of the dough on the prepared pans, leaving lots of space between them. (These suckers spread.) Optional: Place one pecan half on top of each dough mound and press down lightly.

4 Bake one pan at time for 6 minutes, then rotate the pan 180 degrees. Bake for another 6 to 8 minutes, or until the cookies turn golden brown. Immediately remove the parchment from the hot pan and set it on the counter so the cookies stop baking. Allow the cookies to cool on the parchment for 7 minutes, then transfer to a wire rack to cool completely at room temp.

how to WRITE A RECIPE

Here's my process for writing a recipe. Every chef has a different one, but this seems to work for me.

Step 1: I decide what I want to make. Let's say chocolate chip cookies. First, I imagine eating the most perfect chocolate chip cookie. For me, that's a big, super-thin cookie that is brown and crispy on the edges and slightly chewy in the center, and has the perfect ratio of chocolate chips to cookie. Also, it has to have the right amount of salt. Everything needs salt, but chocolate chip cookies especially.

Step 2: I look around for other recipes for thin, crispy chocolate chip cookies. I find two or three. One thing I have noticed when comparing recipes side by side is that for a specific cookie, like a thin and crispy chocolate chip cookie, the ratio of butter to sugar to flour is usually about the same. Of these recipes, I'll pick the one that seems at first glance to be the most like the cookie that I want to bake.

Step 3: I measure all the ingredients, and if the recipe is in cups and spoons, I weigh everything, so I know exactly how many grams everything is. This way, when I start changing things, it's easier to know how much I'm changing them by.

Step 4: I bake the cookies. I make sure I know exactly how hot the oven is, and exactly how long I bake the cookies for. I let the cookies cool, and then I eat them! Fun, right? I have an idea in my head of the cookie I want, and then I compare it to the cookie I have. What's different? I start with the easy stuff. I want less chocolate chips and more salt. Usually, I want more vanilla. Texture is a big thing with me, so I ask if the cookies are crunchy enough on the outside. No? I'll reduce the amount of brown sugar and increase the amount of white sugar. Did they spread out enough? If not, I'll take out a little flour. I write everything down, cross stuff out, make notes, and document the whole process. This way, when I bake these cookies again in six months, I know exactly what to do.

Step 5: I bake the new cookies. If they're perfect, I'll write the recipe down in ink. If not, I repeat step 4 until my recipe is perfect.

And that's how I write a recipe.

THICK
COOKIES

THERE ARE THICK COOKIES, and there are *thick* cookies. Some cookies are thick because they have too much flour and they're kinda cakey. Then there's thick cookies that have the right amount of flour so they don't spread so much in the oven. The trick with thick cookies is knowing exactly how long to bake them. Most thick cookies need to be underbaked, and the difficulty is trusting yourself enough to underbake the cookies on purpose. It is *much* harder to underbake a thick, chewy cookie than to overbake one. It's very easy to overbake a cookie. You know those fudgy chocolate crinkle cookies covered in powdered sugar? Those cookies are amazing when they are baked just enough that the outside holds together. But when you overbake them, the exact same recipe can go from great . . . to garbage. If you find that your cookies are overbaking but you like the color they are on the outside, turn the oven up a little bit. That way you get the color on the outside before the middle has a chance to overbake. A good thick cookie is a bit more difficult to bake well than a good thin cookie, but I believe in you. Let's pour a big glass of milk and make some good thick cookies.

MAKES 24 COOKIES

THUMBPRINT
• COOKIES •

To make food, you have to touch it, and I think Mother Nature stuck the best baking tools to our wrists. These cookies are fun because you jam your thumb into the dough and create a little well for your favorite jam. I like blueberry for this recipe but really any kind of jam or marmalade will work.

INGREDIENTS

1 cup (2 sticks/226 grams)	**butter**, at room temperature
⅓ cup (70 grams)	**granulated sugar**, plus more for rolling
⅓ cup (70 grams)	lightly packed **light brown sugar**
1	**egg yolk**
1 teaspoon	**pure vanilla extract**
2¼ cups (280 grams)	**all-purpose flour**
2 teaspoons	**cornstarch**
Pinch of	**kosher salt**
A jar of	**your favorite jam** (I like blueberry)

❶ In the bowl of a stand mixer fitted with the paddle attachment or in a large bowl using a hand mixer, cream the butter and both sugars. Add the egg yolk and vanilla and mix well, scraping the sides a few times to make sure everything gets mixed in.

❷ In a medium bowl, whisk together the flour, cornstarch, and salt. Sprinkle the flour mixture into the butter mixture and mix until combined. It's a pretty dry dough, so mix it well and keep scraping those sides.

❸ Line two sheet pans with parchment paper. Put some granulated sugar in a small bowl. Scoop tablespoon-size portions of the dough and roll them into balls with your hands. Make sure they're smooth— if there are any cracks, they'll show up when you mash the ball of dough down. Toss each ball in granulated sugar to coat and then place on the prepared pans. Using your thumb, gently press each cookie to make an indentation for the jam. Place the cookies in the freezer for 30 minutes.

❹ Preheat the oven to 375°F.

❺ Take the cookies out of the freezer and fill each thumbprint with jam. Bake the cookies for 10 to 11 minutes, or until the edges start to turn golden brown. Remove from the oven and cool on a wire rack.

White Chocolate
GINGERSNAPS

These gingersnaps have lately become one of my favorite cookies to make. I like *lots* of ginger on mine. Like, lots. Also—very important—these are supposed to be a little soft in the middle, so don't overbake them. Just bake until they look set and matte on the outside.

INGREDIENTS

2 cups (400 grams)	**granulated sugar**, plus more for rolling
1½ cups (327 grams)	**canola oil**
½ cup (140 grams)	**molasses**
2 pinches of	**kosher salt**
2	**large eggs**
4 cups (480 grams)	**all-purpose flour**
4 teaspoons	**baking soda**
3 tablespoons (16 grams)	**ground ginger**
2 teaspoons	**ground cinnamon**
	chopped **white chocolate**
	chopped **crystallized ginger**, for topping

❶ Preheat the oven to 350°F. Line a sheet pan with parchment paper.

❷ In a large bowl, cream the sugar, oil, molasses, and a pinch of kosher salt. Add the eggs one at a time and mix until combined.

❸ In a medium bowl, whisk together the flour, baking soda, ginger, cinnamon, and another pinch of kosher salt. Add the flour mixture to the sugar mixture and beat until just combined. Scrape the bowl during the process and try not to overmix.

❹ Put some sugar in a small bowl. Roll the dough into 1-inch balls and roll each ball in sugar to coat. Place the cookies on the prepared pan. Bake for 10 to 12 minutes, rotating the pans halfway through so the cookies bake evenly. It's really important not to overbake these so the middles stay mushy. Remove from the oven and immediately remove the parchment from the pan and set it on the counter so the cookies stop baking. After 2 minutes, transfer the cookies to a wire rack set over a sheet of parchment to cool completely.

❺ Melt some white chocolate in the microwave (*ew!*) or using a double boiler (*yay!*).

❻ Drizzle the melted white chocolate over the cooled cookies and sprinkle on some crystallized ginger. Use lots of ginger, because when it falls off the cookie, it's like an extra little snack when the cookies are all gone, like the crunchy stuff you get after eating fried fish at Long John Silver's.

Chocolate Peanut Butter

NO-BAKE

· COOKIES ·

INGREDIENTS

½ cup (1 stick/113 grams)	**butter**
⅓ cup (56 grams)	**chocolate chips**
1½ cups (300 grams)	**granulated sugar**
Pinch of	**kosher salt**
½ cup (120 grams)	**whole milk**
2 tablespoons (15 grams)	**unsweetened cocoa powder**
3 cups (230 grams)	**rolled oats**
1 cup (250 grams)	**creamy peanut butter**
2 teaspoons	**pure vanilla extract**

These cookies have a very high ease-to-deliciousness ratio. Super easy to make and super delicious to eat. No-bake cookies are still cookies!

1 In a medium saucepan, melt the butter, chocolate, sugar, salt, milk, and cocoa powder on medium-high heat. Stir with a wooden spoon until it boils. Boil the mixture for exactly 1 minute, then remove from the heat and stir in the oats, peanut butter, and vanilla.

2 Let the mixture sit for 10 minutes so the oats soak up the moisture. Line two sheet pans with parchment paper.

3 Drop 1-tablespoon mounds of cookie dough and gently flatten with the back of a spoon. Chill for 1 hour so they set up. If you want to melt some chocolate and drizzle it on these cookies, you'll get a gold star.

Milk Chocolate
BUTTERSCOTCH
· COOKIES ·

I don't use milk chocolate chips often, but with these sweet butterscotch chips, they're definitely the way to go.

INGREDIENTS

1 cup (2 sticks/226 grams)	**butter**, at room temperature
1¼ cups (226 grams)	lightly packed **dark brown sugar**
½ cup (100 grams)	**granulated sugar**
Big pinch of	**kosher salt**
2	**large eggs**
1 tablespoon (13 grams)	**pure vanilla extract**
1 tablespoon (14 grams)	**baking soda**
3 cups (360 grams)	**all-purpose flour**
1½ cups (255 grams)	**milk chocolate chips**
1½ cups (255 grams)	**butterscotch chips**
1 cup (125 grams)	toasted chopped **pecans** (optional)

1 Preheat the oven to 350°F. Line a few sheet pans with parchment paper.

2 In the bowl of a stand mixer fitted with the paddle attachment, cream the butter, brown sugar, granulated sugar, and salt. Add the eggs and vanilla and mix until smooth.

3 In a medium bowl, whisk the baking soda and flour together, then slowly add the flour mixture to the butter mixture and beat until they are just combined. Add the chocolate chips and butterscotch chips and stir them in by hand so they don't get all mashed up. (If you wanted to add a cup of chopped toasted pecans at this point, I wouldn't tell you not to.)

4 Place 2-tablespoon scoops of cookie dough onto the prepared pans, leaving room between them so the cookies have space to spread out.

5 Bake for 7 to 9 minutes. Remove from the oven and cool on a wire rack. These cookies are best just a tad underbaked.

MAKES 30 COOKIES

Oatmeal Coconut Almond Chocolate BLORBS

My daughter Josephine calls birds "blorbs" and I thought that was the perfect name for these cookies. They're just kinda . . . blorbs. These blorbs are fun because you can really make them your own. Put gummy bears in them, or potato chips, or pretzels. Skittles would be gross, but really colorful.

❶ Preheat the oven to 375°F. Line two sheet pans with parchment paper.

❷ In the bowl of a stand mixer fitted with the paddle attachment or in a large bowl using a hand mixer, cream the butter, brown sugar, and granulated sugar. In a separate bowl, combine the eggs, milk, and vanilla, then incorporate into the creamed butter–sugar mixture and add the flour, baking soda, salt, oats, and coconut. Mix until combined. Add the chocolate chips and almonds and stir them in by hand.

❸ Drop mounds of the dough onto the prepared pans. Gently shape each mound into a half sphere and freeze for 20 minutes.

❹ Bake for 10 to 12 minutes. Remove from the oven and cool on a wire rack.

INGREDIENTS

1 cup (2 sticks/226 grams)	**butter**, at room temperature
1¼ cups (255 grams)	lightly packed **light brown sugar**
½ cup (100 grams)	**granulated sugar**
2	**large eggs**
2 tablespoons (30 grams)	**whole milk**
1 tablespoon (13 grams)	**pure vanilla extract**
1¾ cups (210 grams)	**all-purpose flour**
1 teaspoon	**baking soda**
Pinch of	**kosher salt**
3 cups (240 grams)	**rolled oats**
1 cup (95 grams)	**unsweetened shredded coconut**
2 cups (340 grams)	**chocolate chips**
1 cup (130 grams)	chopped **raw almonds**

My FAVORITE COOKIES

Oreos: I love Oreos the best. I love how crispy the actual cookie part is and how it doesn't shatter and make a big mess when you bite into it. I also like how the Oreo filling basically turns into milk in your mouth, so it's like you're actually eating milk and cookies. Also, original formula only. Double Stuf is too much stuff.

Nutter Butters: My friend Bob and I used to fish a lot when I lived in Sandwich, Massachusetts. We would buy a huge package of Nutter Butters, and we would fish until we finished all the cookies. They're peanut buttery and salty and awesome.

Ice cream cones: I love ice cream cones, because they are usually full of ice cream.

Biscotti: I love the cinnamon sugar on the outside of a biscotti. I also love how dry they are and how they're delicious when you eat them dry, but also totally delicious and totally different and mushy after you dunk them in milky coffee.

Pepperidge Farm Milanos: I like the original dark chocolate Milano cookies. I love putting one in my mouth and curling my tongue around the bottom of it. It's like they were designed specifically for my mouth. They're the perfect cookie.

Florentines: I love how Florentines are super thin but also chewy like candy. I also love chocolate and orange together, and that's the flavor of a Florentine.

Black and Whites: Black and white cookies make me so happy. Not only because they are so big and their texture is more like stale cake than cookie and the frosting is smooth and dry on the outside but soft underneath, but also because I'm usually getting them from a Jewish deli and that means I'm not only having a cookie but also a hot pastrami sandwich and a Dr. Brown's black cherry soda.

Berger Cookies: I love Bergers because they are usually a little smashed when you get them. The frosting has a super-thin, dry layer on the outside. They're also so chocolaty that they are almost more fudgy frosting than a cookie.

Keebler Fudge Stripes: I like how one side is kinda chocolaty and the other side is all chocolaty.

Girl Scout Cookies: I love all Girl Scout Cookies because I love the Girl Scouts, and eating delicious cookies in order to support an awesome organization is a big win all around. If I had to pick a favorite, it would probably be Tagalongs (aka Peanut Butter Patties), followed by Thin Mints as a close second (but only if they're frozen).

Mother's Circus Animal cookies: Get yourself that giant pink sweet-sweet bag, open it, turn on your favorite movie (mine is *Armageddon*), and try to not eat the whole thing at once like it's popcorn. I dare you.

Chewy Chips Ahoy!: I love how they taste almost raw. They taste like they need to bake for a few more minutes, which, in my opinion, means that they're perfect.

Mall cookies: Going to the mall and getting a giant, warm, soft, M&M's-filled Mrs. Fields cookie is absolute bliss.

Royal Dansk Danish butter cookies: Yeah man. That big blue tin filled with all different butter cookies. My favorite one is the pretzel-shaped cookie, because the sugar on it looks like salt.

Little Debbie oatmeal creme pies: I like these because it's two cookies in one package and the weird filling is super sweet. The cookies are real cinnamon-y and so soft, they kinda smear between your tongue and the roof of your mouth.

Nilla wafers: I love Nilla wafers because you make banana pudding with them.

Biscoff cookies: These are fun because they give these out on the airplane, so the only time I eat a Biscoff cookie is when I'm traveling.

Cookie Crisp cereal: Soooo crispy.

Fortune cookies: It's nice to have fortune cookies because it means you just had some clams in black bean sauce and egg rolls and hot-and-sour soup. The cookies themselves aren't very good, but inside they have lottery numbers and little bits of wisdom that you read aloud to the whole table. One time my brother got a fortune that said, "Darth Vader is sleeping under your bed."

MOUND COOKIES

THIN COOKIES ARE THIN, THICK COOKIES ARE THICK, and mound cookies are girthy. They're really thick in the middle and usually have a bunch of *stuff* in them—nuts, fruit, chocolate, even noodles! Mound cookies usually have lots of different textures to them and are endlessly customizable. You can swap in different dried fruits, nuts, and spices to make what you like. Mound cookies are fun and easy to make, too. Open wide!

MAKES 50 COOKIES

POLVORONES

So, there are some pretty specific instructions for these cookies, and the reason is that they have a very particular flavor and texture, and getting all the steps right really makes a difference. They should be crispy all the way through but so tender that they melt in your mouth. You can substitute pecans—or honestly, any nut you wanna use—for the walnuts in this recipe. The *polvorones* I make are really special. They even directly contributed to my wife, Johnna, and me getting married. I think her family liked the cookies so much, they allowed me to marry her.

INGREDIENTS

2½ cups (5 sticks/565 grams)	**butter**
2¼ cups (283 grams)	**walnuts**
4¾ cups (600 grams)	**all-purpose flour**
1¾ cups (214 grams) plus 1 pound (453 grams)	**powdered sugar**
Big pinch of	**kosher salt**
Pinch of	**ground cinnamon**
1½ tablespoons (20 grams)	**pure vanilla extract**

1 Preheat the oven to 350°F. Line a sheet pan with parchment paper.

2 In a medium pot, melt the butter over medium-high heat. It will begin to boil and bubble. Let it, as this is just the water boiling off. Once the butter stops making noise, it will begin to brown. Turn the heat down to medium and keep an eye on it. Stir it around a few times. You'll see little brown flecks appear. This is the milk solids browning. Once you have a nice color and, more important, a nutty, delicious smell, remove the pot from the heat and pour the brown butter into a bowl. Refrigerate it until it's cool. Do not strain it, all those little brown bits are the flavor.

3 Place the walnuts on a sheet pan in one layer. Toast in the oven for 10 to 12 minutes, checking them frequently. You may want to go longer, just don't let the walnuts get too dark or they will be bitter. Remove from the oven and let them cool to room temp. Keep the oven on.

4 Put the cooled walnuts in the bowl of a food processor and buzz until they have the texture of fine gravel. It should be coarser than beach sand but finer than hand-chopped walnuts. Add the brown butter, flour, 1¾ cups (214 grams) of the powdered sugar, the salt, cinnamon, and vanilla, and buzz until combined. Using a small cookie scoop, scoop half spheres of dough onto the prepared pan. Refrigerate until the dough is firm to the touch.

5 Bake for 22 to 25 minutes, rotating the pan 180 degrees after 15 minutes. Remove the cookies from the oven, set the pan on a heat-safe surface, and set a timer for 7 minutes.

6 Put the remaining 1 pound (453 grams) of powdered sugar in a large bowl. When the timer goes off, gently place the warm cookies into the powdered sugar and toss with a fork to generously coat the cookies with sugar. Remove the cookies with a fork (if you touch the cookies, you'll leave a big fingerprint so, you know, don't do that) and put them on a wire rack to cool. They taste much better at room temp than warm. They also keep for weeks, so make lots and enjoy!

Coconut
MACAROONS

INGREDIENTS

1 (14-ounce/(396-gram) bag	**sweetened flaked coconut**
¾ cup plus 2 tablespoons (290 grams)	**sweetened condensed milk**
1 teaspoon	**pure vanilla extract**
2	**egg whites**
Pinch of	**kosher salt**
⅔ cup (113 grams)	**good-quality chocolate**, chopped and melted

These are good out of the cardboard tube on Rosh Hashanah, but man, when they're fresh, they are a whole different animal. Chewy and crispy and super-duper coconutty.

❶ Preheat the oven to 325°F. Line two sheet pans with parchment paper.

❷ In a large bowl, mix together the coconut, condensed milk, and vanilla.

❸ In the bowl of a stand mixer fitted with the whisk attachment or in a large bowl using a hand mixer (or just a whisk, if you're a beast), whip the egg whites and salt to stiff peaks. Don't overwhip! Fold the egg whites into the coconut mixture. Chill the dough in the fridge for 20 minutes.

❹ Using a cookie scoop, place mounds of the mixture onto the prepared pans. Bake for 20 to 25 minutes, or until the coconut pieces sticking out of the cookies start to brown. Remove from the oven and cool on a wire rack.

❺ Dip the cooled cookies in the melted chocolate and place them on a clean piece of parchment. Refrigerate for 10 minutes so the chocolate sets up, then enjoy.

I USED TO HATE MACAROONS

~~~~~~~~~~~~~~~~~~

I grew up thinking macaroons were the worst. They came in these cardboard tubes that had a metal rim that you would always scratch yourself on. They were somehow soft and limp and pale but also dry at the same time. One year for Passover, I decided "enough already," and made them from scratch. When I took my first bite, the clouds parted, the sun shone bright, and I could hear the ringing of trumpets far off in the distance. These cookies were delicious! Then one year, I went to a friend's house for Passover, and they had the cardboard tube. At first, I was dismayed, but it had been so long since I had had one of the factory-made ones that I was curious to see if they were as bad as I remembered. I picked one up and took a sniff and popped it in my mouth. Instantly, I was transported back to my childhood. The flavor of that dry, pale macaroon was the flavor of Passover and Hebrew school and my grandma's house. Now every year I bake my delicious chocolate-dipped crispy-chewy macaroons *and* I get a tube of the store-bought ones—all to remind myself that just because something is "bad" doesn't mean it's *bad*.

MAKES 30 COOKIES

HAYSTACK
• COOKIES •

INGREDIENTS

2 cups (340 grams)	**white chocolate chips**
2 cups (340 grams)	**butterscotch chips**
1 cup (250 grams)	**peanut butter** (smooth or chunky— your call, chef)
12 ounces (340 grams)	**crunchy chow mein noodles**

Who puts noodles in cookies?! That's so weird! I know, it's super weird, but just give it a try. This recipe takes like 5 seconds. If you don't like it, no big whoop. But—spoiler alert—you will.

1 Line a sheet pan with parchment paper.

2 Melt the white chocolate chips and butterscotch chips together using a double boiler. Add the peanut butter and stir until the mixture is smooth. Add the chow mein noodles (and anything else you want) and stir to coat.

3 Form the mixture into mounds on the prepared pan and chill in the fridge for 15 minutes to set before enjoying.

WHAT ARE DROP COOKIES?

~~~~~~~~~~

There are so many kinds of cookies. Bar cookies are baked in a pan and cut after they cool. Rolled cookies are rolled out with a rolling pin and cut out. There's sandwich cookies, cream cookies, refrigerator cookies, no-bake cookies, even computer cookies! Drop cookies are cookies that you spoon up, drop on a sheet pan, and bake. The heat in the oven melts the dough so the cookies bake flat. I think drop cookies are the easiest ones to make. You just turn on the oven, drop the cookie dough, and let heat and gravity do the work. Drop cookies don't bake into perfect circles. They end up with all kinds of weird curves that give them their personality—and the nice thing about drop cookies is that with all the irregularities, you get more edges, which (in my opinion) are the best part of the cookie!

MAKES 36 COOKIES

Oatmeal NUGS

There are two types of people in the world: chewy oatmeal cookie people and crispy oatmeal cookie people. These cookies are great because they're crispy on the outside and chewy in the middle. So if you like crispy oatmeal cookies, you'll like these. And if you like chewy oatmeal cookies, you'll like these. Therefore, everyone in the world loves this recipe. Be excellent to each other.

1 In a medium bowl, combine the flour, baking soda, cinnamon, and salt.

2 In the bowl of a stand mixer fitted with the paddle attachment or in a large bowl using a hand mixer, cream the butter and both sugars. Beat in the eggs one at a time, then the vanilla. Add the flour mixture and beat until combined. Add the oats, pecans, chocolate chips, and raisins and stir them in by hand. Chill the dough in the fridge for about an hour.

3 Preheat the oven to 375°F. Line two sheet pans with parchment paper.

4 Scoop about 1 tablespoon of the dough onto the prepared pans, making sure to leave a little space between each cookie. Bake for 12 to 15 minutes, or until the edges start to turn brown but the middles are still somewhat pale. Remove from the oven and cool on a wire rack.

INGREDIENTS

1¾ cups (224 grams)	**all-purpose flour**
1 teaspoon	**baking soda**
2 teaspoons	**ground cinnamon**
Pinch of	**kosher salt**
1 cup (2 sticks/227 grams)	**butter**, at room temperature
1 cup (200 grams)	lightly packed **brown sugar**
½ cup (90 grams)	**granulated sugar**
2	**large eggs**
2 teaspoons	**pure vanilla extract**
4 cups (300 grams)	**rolled oats**
1 cup (100 grams)	chopped **pecans**, lightly toasted
1 cup (175 grams)	**chocolate chips**
½ cup (100 grams)	**raisins**

Double Chocolate DROP

• COOKIES •

Chocolate chip cookies are great, but sometimes you just need *more* chocolate. These cookies scratch that itch. It's a chocolaty cookie that is filled with chocolate chips. And if you want to throw in some chopped toasted walnuts, these cookies can get even better.

1 Preheat the oven to 375°F. Line two sheet pans with parchment paper.

2 In a medium bowl, whisk together the flour, cocoa powder, baking soda, and salt.

3 In the bowl of a stand mixer fitted with the paddle attachment or in a large bowl using a hand mixer, cream together the butter and both sugars. Add the egg and vanilla and beat until combined. Give the bowl a good scrape. Add the flour mixture and beat on low until combined. Stir in the chocolate chips by hand.

4 With a medium cookie scoop, make balls of dough and place them on the prepared pans about 2 inches apart so they don't melt into each other. Chill in the freezer for 20 minutes.

5 Bake the cookies for 10 minutes, or until the centers just turn dry. Don't overbake. Remove from the oven and cool on a wire rack.

⟩ INGREDIENTS ⟩

1 cup (120 grams)	**all-purpose flour**
⅓ cup (33 grams)	**unsweetened cocoa powder**
1 teaspoon	**baking soda**
Pinch of	**kosher salt**
½ cup (1 stick/113 grams)	**butter**, at room temperature
½ cup (110 grams)	lightly packed **light brown sugar**
⅓ cup (110 grams)	**granulated sugar**
1	**large egg**
2 teaspoons	**pure vanilla extract**
1 cup (180 grams)	**semisweet chocolate chips**

INTERN COOKIES

ATIONAL

THERE ARE SO MANY PLACES OUT THERE! And every place has its own cookies. Around the world, cookies come in different shapes and textures, using different spices and other ingredients. You can learn a lot about people by what kind of cookies they make. Travel the world. Eat cookies.

Cookies from

AROUND THE WORLD

1
CANADA
Nanaimo bars

2
UNITED STATES
Whoopie pies

3
MEXICO
Coyotas

4
GUATEMALA
Champurradas

5
CHILE
Cuchuflí

6
BRAZIL
Brigadeiros

7
SWITZERLAND
Zimtsterne

8
SPAIN
Pastissets

9
PORTUGAL
Cavacas de Margaride

11 GERMANY Vanillekipferl

12 NORWAY Krumkake

13 FINLAND Joulutorttu

29 RUSSIA Zefir

10 ENGLAND Jammy Dodgers

14 SLOVAKIA Medovníky

16 CZECH REPUBLIC Kolaches

15 GREECE Koulourakia

17 CROATIA Rafioli

18 BOSNIA Šape

19 IRAN Koloocheh

30 SOUTH KOREA Hodugwaja

31 JAPAN Manju

22 ITALY Pignoli

21 ALGERIA Makroud

20 MOROCCO Fekkas

23 CORSICA Canistrelli

24 EGYPT Kahk

26 ISRAEL Tahini cookies

27 IRAQ Kleicha

25 JORDAN Ghraybeh

28 INDIA Nankhatai

32 PHILIPPINES Silvanas

33 INDONESIA Nastar

34 AUSTRALIA Anzac biscuits

35 NEW ZEALAND Milk Chocolate Roughs

MAKES 50
COOKIES

Chinese
ALMOND
· COOKIES ·

Chinese almond cookies aren't actually Chinese, but, like the fortune cookie, they were invented by Chinese bakers in America (today some of the best almond cookies are manufactured in Hong Kong). They have a light, crispy texture and a nutty almond flavor that works pretty well at the end of a big Chinese meal. They are also now traditionally served during Lunar New Year and are round to symbolize coins and good luck.

❶ In the bowl of a stand mixer fitted with the paddle attachment, beat together the butter, almond flour, and a pinch of salt. Add 1 egg and the almond extract. Beat until combined.

❷ In a medium bowl, whisk together the all-purpose flour, sugar, and baking soda. Add the flour mixture to the butter mixture and beat until combined. The dough will look dry and crumbly. Dump the dough onto the counter and mush it together with your hands. Flatten the dough into a disc, wrap it in plastic wrap, and put it in the fridge for 2 hours.

❸ Preheat the oven the 325°F. Line three sheet pans with parchment paper.

❹ Roll the dough into roughly ¾-inch balls with your hands. Place them about 2 inches apart on the prepared pans. Put a few drops of water on your fingertips and gently press each ball of dough down until it looks like a thick disc.

❺ Whisk the remaining egg in a small bowl with a pinch of salt and a pinch of sugar to make an egg wash. (This helps the white and yolk become one.) Press an almond into the center of each cookie. With a pastry brush, brush each cookie with the egg wash. Bake for 12 to 15 minutes, or until the edges turn golden brown. Remove from the oven and cool on a wire rack.

INGREDIENTS

1 cup (2 sticks/226 grams)	cold **butter**, cut into cubes
1⅓ cups (150 grams)	**almond flour**
Pinch of	**kosher salt**
2	**large eggs**
1 teaspoon	**almond extract**
1¾ cups (210 grams)	**all-purpose flour**
1 cup plus 2 tablespoons (220 grams)	**granulated sugar**, plus a pinch
½ teaspoon	**baking soda**
	blanched whole almonds

International Cookies **69**

MOONCAKES

If you want to make mooncakes, you have to really *want* to make mooncakes. There are a few things you need that you probably don't have in your kitchen. You need a mooncake mold, traditionally made from wood. If you don't want to get one, you can use a mini-muffin tin for these cookies. They won't look as cool, but they'll still be delicious. You will also need golden syrup, lye water (or alkaline water), adzuki beans (red mung beans), and malt sugar. You can get all these online, but if you have an Asian grocery store near you and you have never been, I encourage you to go.

INGREDIENTS

FOR THE FILLING

9 tablespoons (100 grams)	**dried adzuki beans** (red mung beans)
3 tablespoons (40 grams)	**vegetable oil**
7 tablespoons (80 grams)	**granulated sugar**
1 tablespoon (15 grams)	**malt sugar**
Pinch of	**kosher salt**

FOR THE DOUGH

½ cup (150 grams)	**golden syrup**
½ teaspoon	**lye water**
4 tablespoons (60 grams)	**vegetable oil**
Pinch of	**kosher salt**
2 cups (250 grams)	**cake flour**
2	**egg yolks**
¼ cup (60 grams)	**whole milk**

MAKE THE FILLING

❶ Soak the adzuki beans in water to cover overnight. Drain the beans and put them in a pot. Cover the beans with fresh water and simmer, covered, for 2½ hours, or until the beans are soft. Drain them and let them cool.

❷ Put the cooled beans in the bowl of a food processor and add the oil, granulated sugar, malt sugar, and salt and process until smooth. Cover and set aside.

MAKE THE DOUGH

❸ In a medium bowl, mix the golden syrup and the lye water. Add the oil and salt and whisk until combined.

❹ Sift the cake flour and add it to the mixture. Mix well to form a dough. Wrap the dough in plastic wrap and let rest at room temperature for 30 minutes.

❺ Preheat the oven to 350°F. Line a sheet pan with parchment paper.

❻ Divide the dough into 20 equal portions and roll each into a smooth ball. Cover the balls with plastic wrap. Working with one ball at a time (and keeping the others covered), roll out the dough really thin, like ⅛ inch thick, and place about 1½ tablespoons of the filling in the center. Wrap the dough around the filling and pinch the edges to seal. Lightly flour the dough ball and a mooncake mold. Press the ball into the mold, then gently tap the mold on the counter to release the mooncake. Place the mooncake on the prepared pan and repeat with the remaining dough and filling.

7 Whisk together the egg yolks and milk in a small bowl to make an egg wash. Gently brush the mooncakes with the egg wash and remove any excess with a clean paper towel; reserve the remaining egg wash. Bake the mooncakes for 10 to 12 minutes, or until golden brown. Remove from the oven and cool for 5 minutes, then brush gently with egg wash again. The residual heat will cook the egg wash. Let the cookies cool completely.

8 Store the mooncakes in an airtight container at room temperature for 1 to 2 days. You want to give the oils in the dough time to rise to the surface of the mooncakes so they become shiny. Trust me, they're better after 48 hours.

Cardamom Pistachio
LADDU

INGREDIENTS

¾ cup (97 grams)	**shelled pistachios**
½ cup (100 grams)	**granulated sugar**
3 tablespoons (42 grams)	**butter**
1 (14-ounce/(397-gram) can	**sweetened condensed milk**
2¼ cups (214 grams)	**unsweetened flaked coconut**
Pinch of	**kosher salt**
2 teaspoons	**ground cardamom**

My good friend Kulin introduced me to these unique Indian cookies when I was in college. The store-bought kind sometimes come in a cardboard box with beautiful pictures on it. They have a texture like nothing else I have ever tried, kind of sweet and crumbly but super tender and moist. If you have never heard of cardamom, I promise you will like it. It's the flavor in Apple Jacks cereal.

1 Put the pistachios in the bowl of a food processor and pulse until you get a fine powder. In a small bowl, mix 1½ teaspoons of the pistachio powder with the sugar. Set the rest of the pistachio powder aside.

2 In a sauté pan, combine the butter and condensed milk and heat over medium heat to melt the butter. Stir with a wooden spoon to combine. Dump in the coconut, the remaining pistachio powder, and the salt. Turn the heat down to medium-low and cook, stirring constantly, until the mixture comes together and gets really thick, about 10 minutes. When the mixture looks almost done, stir in the cardamom. Remove from the heat and let cool slightly.

3 When the mixture has cooled enough to handle but is still warm, form it into balls and then roll them in the pistachio sugar to coat. Place the balls on a sheet pan and let cool to room temperature, then enjoy. I like leaving them uncovered for a few hours so the outside dries out, because I like that texture.

KANOM PING

These cookies were invented by a Japanese Portuguese Bengali chef who was working in Thailand. She used a traditional Portuguese recipe and adapted it to use local ingredients—in this case, tapioca starch. These cookies have the coolest texture, and they literally melt in your mouth. Usually when you buy these cookies packaged in Thailand (I have never seen them in America), they are pretty hard. The ones you make at home are so much more delicate and the only way to really experience the yumminess.

INGREDIENTS

1½ cups (342 grams)	coconut milk
½ cup (100 grams)	granulated sugar
1 tablespoon (8 grams)	ground ginger
Pinch of	kosher salt
2	egg yolks
2 cups (260 grams)	tapioca starch
	food coloring
⅓ cup (57 grams)	white chocolate, chopped and melted
	crystallized ginger, super thinly sliced

❶ In a medium saucepot, combine the coconut milk, sugar, ground ginger, and salt. Bring to a boil over medium-high heat, then reduce the heat to maintain a simmer and cook for 25 minutes or so, until the mixture thickens. It won't be like chewing gum or anything, but it also shouldn't be watery. Remove the pot from the heat and let the mixture cool until just warm, then whisk in the egg yolk.

❷ Dump the tapioca starch into a bowl and make a well in the middle. Pour the coconut mixture into the well and stir with a fork. When the dough is too solid to mix with the fork, remove it from the bowl and knead it with your hands until it comes together. Divide the dough into however many colors you want and tint each ball with food coloring. These are traditionally very lightly colored, so use just a few drops. Wrap the dough balls in plastic wrap and let them rest at room temp for 30 minutes.

❸ Preheat the oven to 350°F. Line two sheet pans with parchment paper.

❹ Roll the dough into little marble-size balls and place them on the prepared pans. Bake for 25 to 30 minutes, until just the bottoms start to turn brown. Turn the oven off, crack the oven door open, and allow the cookies to cool completely in the oven.

❺ Melt the white chocolate in a saucepan over medium-low heat. Remove the cooled cookies from the oven. Dip the ends of the crystallized ginger pieces into the melted chocolate and stick them to the top of the cookies.

ALFAJORES

Alfajores are sandwich cookies that come from Central and South America by way of Spain by way of ancient Persia. They have an incredible history and an even more incredible texture, like no other cookie I know. They are buttery but also light and crispy but also tender. I know, makes no sense. Just give these a try—you'll totally see what I mean.

INGREDIENTS

1½ cups (200 grams)	**all-purpose flour**
2 cups plus 2 tablespoons (300 grams)	**cornstarch**
2 teaspoons	**baking powder**
1 teaspoon	**baking soda**
¾ cup plus 2 tablespoons (1¾ sticks/200 grams)	**butter**, at room temperature
1¼ cups (150 grams)	**powdered sugar**
3	**egg yolks**
2 teaspoons	**pure vanilla extract**
1½ cups (350 grams)	**dulce de leche**
½ cup (48 grams)	**unsweetened shredded coconut** (optional)

1 In a medium bowl, whisk together the flour, cornstarch, baking powder, and baking soda.

2 In the bowl of a stand mixer fitted with the paddle attachment or in a large bowl using a hand mixer, cream the butter and powdered sugar. Add the egg yolks and the vanilla and beat until smooth. Add the flour mixture and beat until just combined. Do not overmix! The texture of these cookies is magical and overmixing can make them, uh, Muggles. Form the dough into a flat disc, wrap in plastic wrap, and chill it in the fridge for an hour or so.

3 Roll the dough out to about ¼ inch thick. Cut the dough into 4 pieces and stack them, with a piece of parchment between each piece of dough. Place in the fridge for 15 minutes.

4 Preheat the oven to 350°F. Line two sheet pans with parchment paper.

5 Using a 2-inch fluted cookie cutter, cut out cookies from the chilled dough and gently place them on the prepared pans. Freeze for at least 15 minutes before baking.

6 Bake for 8 to 10 minutes, or until the cookies begin to turn golden brown at the edges. Remove from the oven and cool on a wire rack.

7 Put a little less than a tablespoon of dulce de leche on the flat side of half the cookies, then sandwich with the remaining cookies. Press down on the sandwiched cookie until the filling juuuuust comes to the edge. Optional: Place the coconut in a small bowl, then roll the cookie in the coconut so it sticks to the filling along the edge.

MAKES 24 COOKIES

BISCOTTI

INGREDIENTS

1 cup (130 grams)	**almonds**
3½ cups (420 grams)	**all-purpose flour**
1 teaspoon	**baking powder**
1 teaspoon	**baking soda**
2 teaspoons	**ground cinnamon**
Pinch of	**kosher salt**
4	**large eggs**
¾ cup (150 grams)	**granulated sugar**
¼ cup (40 grams)	lightly packed **brown sugar**
1 teaspoon	**almond extract**
¾ cup (110 grams)	chopped **dried apricots**
	chopped **chocolate**, for decorating

When I was a kid, I always thought biscotti were these weird Italian cookies for adults that probably tasted like walnut shells. When I eventually tried them, I realized I was totally wrong. They're crunchy and chewy at the same time, and I find them to be really substantial, like a cookie-as-a-meal kinda thing. They're fun to dip in Yoo-hoo, too.

1 Preheat the oven to 350°F. Line two sheet pans with parchment.

2 Spread the almonds on a sheet pan and toast in the oven for 12 minutes. Remove from the oven and let cool. Chop them into pieces with a knife. Set aside.

3 In a medium bowl, whisk together the flour, baking powder, baking soda, cinnamon, and salt. In another bowl, whisk together the eggs, both sugars, and the almond extract. Pour the egg mixture into the flour mixture and stir to combine. Add the toasted almonds and apricots and fold them into the dough.

4 Divide the dough in half and roll each piece into a log about 10 inches long. Place one log on each prepared pan. Gently press the top of the log so it flattens just a little bit. Bake for 15 minutes, or until a rich golden brown. Remove from the oven and let cool for 10 minutes; keep the oven on.

5 Use a serrated knife to cut the logs crosswise into ¼- to ½-inch-wide segments. Take your time and cut straight! Lay the segments flat on the sheet pans, cut-side up, and bake them for 10 minutes. Remove from the oven, flip each cookie, and bake for another 10 minutes. Remove from the oven and cool on a wire rack set over a sheet of parchment paper.

6 Melt some chocolate in the microwave (*ew!*) or using a double boiler (*yay!*) and drizzle it onto the cookies.

PRO TIP: If you chop the apricots and then toss them in a little flour, they won't all stick together when you are folding them into the dough.

MAKES 24 COOKIES

TAHINI
• COOKIES •

INGREDIENTS

2 cups (240 grams)	**all-purpose flour**
1 teaspoon	**baking powder**
¾ cup (1½ sticks/170 grams)	**butter**, at room temperature
¾ cup (150 grams)	**granulated sugar**
3 tablespoons (64 grams)	**honey**
¾ cup (180 grams)	**tahini**
Pinch of	**kosher salt**
¼ cup (35 grams)	**sesame seeds**, toasted

The first time I had these cookies was at a market in Israel. The bakery was right next door to the stall where the guy was grinding the sesame seeds into tahini. That's about as fresh as it gets. They're really fun and the whole sesame seeds on the outside make the texture really incredible. BTW, there's a kind of sesame candy made from tahini called halvah—if you ever see it, give it a try, if you haven't yet. It is so delicious and one of the most unique textures I have ever eaten. It's like a cross between peanut butter and oil shale.

1 Preheat the oven to 350°F. Line two sheet pans with parchment paper.

2 In a medium bowl, whisk together the flour and baking powder.

3 In the bowl of a stand mixer fitted with the paddle attachment or in a large bowl using a hand mixer, cream the butter, sugar, honey, tahini, and salt. Add the flour mixture to the butter mixture in three additions and beat to combine.

4 Pour the sesame seeds into a small bowl. Scoop out 1-ounce portions of dough and roll them into balls with your hands. Dip the balls into the sesame seeds and place them on the prepared pans, sesame-seed-side up. (You can also coat the entire cookie in sesame seeds. I like the weird bottom sesame seeds personally.)

5 Bake for 12 to 13 minutes, or until the cookies start to turn golden brown. Remove from the oven and cool on a wire rack.

PFEFFERNUESSE

The name literally means "pepper nuts" in German. These cookies don't have any nuts in them, but they're the size of a medium walnut and have a nice kick of white pepper to them. If you have pink peppercorns, they work absolutely great in these. (They're also nice as a little garnish.) I know ground pepper in a cookie might sound weird, but give these a shot.

INGREDIENTS

FOR THE DOUGH

2¼ cups (270 grams)	**all-purpose flour**
½ teaspoon	**baking soda**
4 teaspoons	**Lebkuchengewürz** (a German spice blend that you can find online or in specialty grocery stores)
Pinch of	**kosher salt**
¼ teaspoon	**ground white pepper**
¼ cup (28 grams)	**almond flour**
½ cup (107 grams)	**brown sugar**
5 tablespoons (70 grams)	**butter**, at room temperature
⅓ cup (113 grams)	**honey**
3 tablespoons (45 grams)	**heavy cream**
1	**large egg**

FOR THE GLAZE

2½ cups (325 grams)	**powdered sugar**
¾ tablespoon	**skim milk**
50	**whole pink peppercorns**

MAKE THE DOUGH

1 In a medium bowl, mix the flour, baking soda, Lebkuchengewürz, salt, pepper, and almond flour.

2 In a medium pot, combine the brown sugar, butter, honey, and cream. Heat over medium heat, stirring, until melted and smooth, then remove from the heat. Let sit for 5 minutes and then stir in the flour mixture. Add the egg and stir until combined. The dough will be sticky and shiny. Wrap the dough in plastic wrap and chill it in the fridge overnight.

3 Preheat the oven to 350°F. Line a sheet pan with parchment paper.

4 Roll the dough into 1-tablespoon balls and place on the prepared pan. Work with a small amount of dough at a time, keeping the rest in the fridge so it doesn't get too warm. Bake for 13 to 15 minutes, or until golden brown. Remove from the oven and cool on a wire rack.

MAKE THE GLAZE

5 While the cookies are cooling, whisk together the powdered sugar and skim milk. Dip the cooled cookies into the glaze, sprinkle with a little pink peppercorn, and return them to the rack until the glaze hardens.

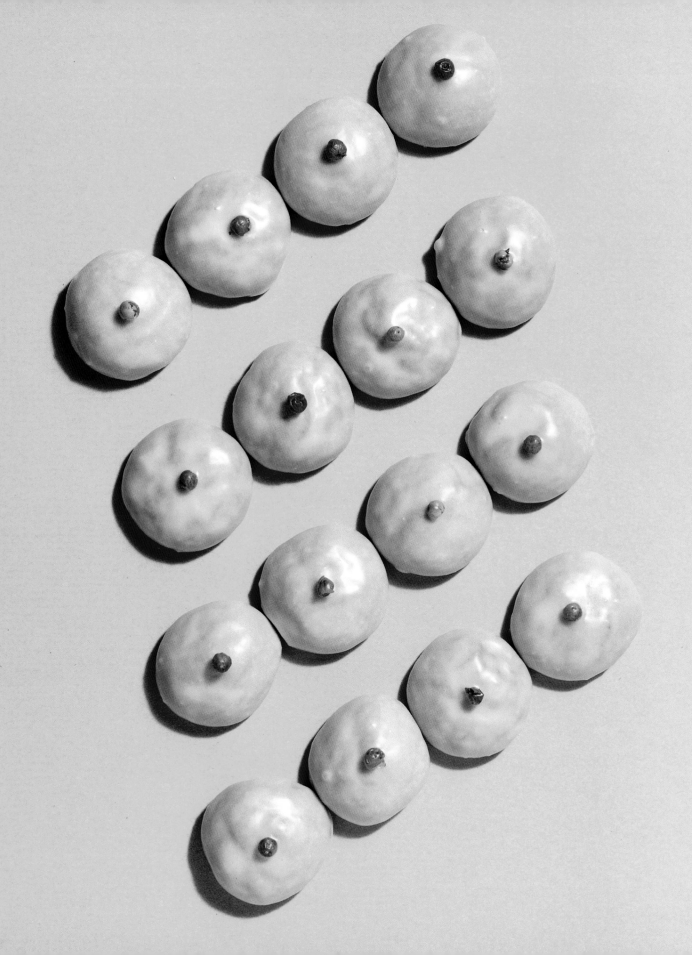

MAKES 12 COOKIES

TORTAS DE ACEITE

INGREDIENTS

2 teaspoons	**active dry yeast**
⅔ cup (160 grams)	**warm water**
3 tablespoons (38 grams)	**granulated sugar**
2½ cups (300 grams)	**Italian "00" flour** (the flour traditionally used for pasta in Italy) or **cake flour**
Pinch of	**kosher salt**
2 teaspoons	**fennel seeds**
½ cup (109 grams)	**extra-virgin olive oil**
	powdered sugar, for dusting
1	**egg white,** beaten

These are a really unique Spanish cookie. They are flat and crispy and kinda blur the line between sweet and savory and cookie and cracker. They're really flaky and also a little messy to eat, which to me is always a good sign.

1 Preheat the oven to 450°F.

2 Pour the yeast into the warm water, add a pinch of the granulated sugar, whisk, and cover with a paper towel. Let stand for 10 minutes, or until it gets frothy and smells like a bakery.

3 In a bowl, mix 1½ cups (180 grams) of the flour, the salt, and the fennel seeds. Make a well in the center of the flour mixture and pour in the oil and the yeast mixture. Start stirring with a fork until the dough comes together. If the dough is too sticky to mix with your hands, add a little flour at a time until you can handle the dough but it's not too dry. Cover the dough and let it rest at room temperature for 10 minutes.

4 Line a sheet pan with parchment paper and lightly oil the parchment, then dust it with powdered sugar.

5 Divide the dough into 12 equal pieces and roll them into balls. Roll out each ball with a rolling pin until the dough is so thin, you can almost see through it. Place the cookies on the prepared pan and brush lightly with the egg white. Dust the tops with powdered sugar and then sprinkle a little of the granulated sugar on each one.

6 Bake for 5 to 10 minutes, or until they are golden brown and crisp. They burn really fast, so keep a close eye on them. Eat 'em warm!

MAKES 25 COOKIES

Scottish
SHORTBREAD

There really is nothing like the flavor and texture of good Scottish shortbread. It's so buttery, slightly sweet, slightly salty, and simple. I also find that shortbread is better after it sits for 24 to 48 hours rather than served fresh.

INGREDIENTS

2¾ cups (340 grams)	**all-purpose flour**
1 cup (125 grams)	**powdered sugar**
1½ teaspoons	**kosher salt**
1 cup (2 sticks/225 grams)	**European butter**, at room temperature

1 Sift the flour and powdered sugar together into a large bowl. Whisk in the salt. Add the butter and work it into the flour-sugar mixture until a crumbly dough forms.

2 Knead the cookie dough on the counter until it becomes smooth, then form into a ball. Wrap in plastic wrap and chill in the fridge for an hour.

3 Preheat the oven to 300°F.

4 Roll out the dough to ½ inch thick, then roll the whole sheet of dough into a shortbread pan and trim to fit. Pierce the tops of the cookies with a fork so they don't bubble as they bake. If you want cool patterns on the top (like you see here), try using a cookie mold. It shouldn't make it taste better, but somehow I think it does.

5 Bake for 45 minutes, or until evenly golden brown. Let cool on the pan for 10 minutes, then turn the shortbread out of the pan and carefully cut it into individual cookies with a serrated knife. Cool completely before eating.

SANDW
COOKIES

ICH

SANDWICH COOKIES ARE THE BEST.
You get two cookies in every cookie and some kind of creamy, yummy filling. The trick is making the individual cookies all the same size so you don't get weird sandwiches where the filling is exposed or there's just a little blob of filling. So watch that.

MAKES 28 COOKIES

FLORENTINES

Florentines are really special cookies. Super thin and crispy but also kinda chewy. One of my favorite flavor combinations is orange and chocolate, and it is magical in these cookies. You don't have to make these cookies into sandwiches—they're great to eat individually as well.

INGREDIENTS

2 cups (260 grams)	**sliced almonds**, roughly chopped
2 tablespoons (15 grams)	**all-purpose flour**
2 teaspoons	minced **orange zest**
Pinch of	**kosher salt**
¾ cup (150 grams)	**granulated sugar**
½ cup (1 stick/113 grams)	**butter**
⅓ cup (80 grams)	**heavy cream**
2 tablespoons (42 grams)	**honey**
2 teaspoons	**pure vanilla extract**
1⅓ cups (226 grams)	**dark chocolate chips**

❶ Preheat the oven to 350°F. Line two sheet pans with parchment paper.

❷ In a medium bowl, mix the almonds, flour, orange zest, and salt.

❸ In a medium saucepan, combine the sugar, butter, heavy cream, and honey. Bring to a boil over medium heat, then remove from the heat. Let cool for 20 minutes and then stir in the almond mixture and the vanilla.

❹ Spoon the batter onto the prepared pans, using about 2 tablespoons for each cookie and leaving plenty of space around each. These cookies spread a lot. Flatten each cookie with your fingers and try to keep them round. Bake for 10 minutes, or until golden brown on the edges and slightly brown in the middle. Remove from the oven and cool on a wire rack.

❺ Melt the chocolate in the microwave (*ew!*) or using a double boiler (*yay!*). Spread a thin, even layer over the flat side of one cookie and place another cookie on top to form a sandwich. Repeat to fill the remaining cookies, drizzle the rest of the melted chocolate over the cookies, and then let them set for about 5 minutes before eating.

STROOPWAFELS

First of all, it's fun to say "stroopwafel" in a Dutch accent. Second of all, fresh stroopwafels are some of the most delicious things I've ever had. When they're warm, the inside is all molasses-y and gooey. The outside has a texture that's somewhere between an ice cream cone and a Waffle House waffle. (And if you've never been to Waffle House, go. Now. And get the grits.) You'll need a waffle iron for this recipe.

INGREDIENTS

FOR THE COOKIES

¾ tablespoon (10 grams)	**active dry yeast**
1 tablespoon (15 grams)	warm **whole milk**
½ cup (1 stick/113 grams)	**butter**, at room temperature
½ cup (100 grams)	**granulated sugar**
1	**large egg**, beaten
2¼ cups (270 grams)	**cake flour** (**all-purpose flour** also works, but the cookies won't be as crispy on the outside)
Pinch of	**kosher salt**

FOR THE FILLING

10 tablespoons (175 grams)	**blackstrap molasses**
¾ cup (150 grams)	lightly packed **light brown sugar**
½ cup (1 stick/113 grams)	**butter**
1 teaspoon	**ground cinnamon**

MAKE THE COOKIES

① Preheat the oven to 150°F and put a sheet pan in there to warm up, too.

② Put the yeast and the warm milk in a bowl and cover with a clean kitchen towel. (Before you add the yeast, make sure the milk isn't too hot—it should be just slightly warmer than room temp.) Let sit for about 7 minutes, until bubbling and foamy.

③ In a bowl, stir together the butter, granulated sugar, and egg with a wooden spoon. Pour in the yeast mixture and stir it all together. Mix in the flour and the salt, stirring gently but combining them completely. Cover the dough with a warm, moist towel and let it rise for about an hour.

WHILE THE DOUGH IS RISING, MAKE THE FILLING

④ In a medium pot, combine the molasses, brown sugar, butter, and cinnamon and heat over medium-low heat, stirring, until the mixture is smooth. Remove from the heat.

⑤ Get the hot sheet pan out of the oven and put a piece of parchment paper on it. Roll the dough into Ping-Pong-ball-size balls. While the sheet pan is still warm to the touch, place the dough balls on there. Cover with a warm, moist towel and let them rise for 15 minutes.

⑥ Grease and heat your waffle iron. Place a ball of dough in the waffle iron, press down, and cook for 2 minutes (if you're using an open-flame waffle iron) or 3 minutes (if you're using an electric one), until the dough is golden brown. Remove the waffle cookie from the waffle iron.

7 **THIS IS IMPORTANT:** While the cookie is still hot, cut it in half lengthwise through the middle. Spread some of the filling over one half in a thin layer. Not too much! It's a strong flavor and you don't want a lot. Press the top half back on and serve. Repeat with the rest of the dough and filling. Eating these immediately is the best, but they will still be delicious after 24 hours.

OH-WEE-OHS

Oreos are my favorite cookie. I love them from the package. I developed this recipe because I wanted to see if I could make them myself. Turns out, I can. I probably won't make these cookies every time I want an Oreo, but it's nice to know I have the option.

INGREDIENTS

FOR THE COOKIES

¼ cup (½ stick/58 grams)	**butter**, at room temperature
½ cup (100 grams)	**granulated sugar**
3 tablespoons (55 grams)	**light corn syrup**
½ teaspoon	**pure vanilla extract**
1¼ cups (165 grams)	**all-purpose flour**
Heaping ⅓ cup (35 grams)	**unsweetened cocoa powder**, plus more for dusting
1 teaspoon	**baking soda**
Pinch of	**kosher salt**

FOR THE FILLING

¾ cup (175 grams)	**vegetable shortening**, melted
2 cups (240 grams)	**powdered sugar**
Pinch of	**kosher salt**
1 teaspoon	**pure vanilla extract**

MAKE THE COOKIES

❶ In a large bowl, cream the butter, granulated sugar, corn syrup, and vanilla until light and smooth.

❷ In a separate bowl, whisk together the flour, cocoa powder, baking soda, and salt. Add the flour mixture to the butter mixture and mix until the dough comes together. You may need to knead it by hand for a bit. Divide the dough in half, form each portion into a disc, wrap each disc in plastic wrap, and chill them in the fridge for 30 minutes.

❸ Preheat the oven to 350°F. Line a sheet pan with parchment paper.

❹ Dust the dough with cocoa powder and roll it out until it's ⅛ inch thick. Using a cutter, cut 1½-inch rounds from the dough. Arrange them relatively close together on the prepared pan, poke each round with a fork, and freeze for 15 minutes.

❺ Bake for 12 to 15 minutes, or until the cookies look dried out. Remove from the oven and cool on a wire rack.

MAKE THE FILLING

❻ Pour the shortening into the bowl of a stand mixer fitted with the paddle attachment. Add the powdered sugar, salt, and vanilla. Beat until soft and smooth. You have to use this immediately as it sets up pretty fast.

❼ Fill a pastry bag with the filling or use a small scoop. Spread the filling over the flat side of half the cookies and sandwich with the remaining cookies. Fill and assemble one sandwich cookie at a time so the filling doesn't set too fast.

MAKES 12 COOKIES

S'MORE
• COOKIES •

S'mores are great, but sometimes making them requires more work than you're willing to put in. These cookies are a great compromise. They have chocolate, marshmallows, and graham crackers all in one cookie. I think they're genius, if I do say so myself.

❶ In a medium bowl, whisk together the all-purpose flour, whole wheat flour, cinnamon, baking soda, and salt.

❷ In the bowl of a stand mixer fitted with the paddle attachment or in a large bowl using a hand mixer, cream the butter and both sugars. Add the egg, egg yolk, and vanilla and beat until combined, then add the flour mixture and beat some more. Stir in half the chocolate chips by hand. Cover the dough and chill in the fridge for at least an hour.

❸ Preheat the oven to 375°F. Line four sheet pans with parchment paper.

❹ Scoop the dough using a medium cookie scoop, putting 6 scoops on each prepared pan. Bake for 10 to 12 minutes, or until the cookies start to turn golden brown. Remove from the oven and cool on a wire rack.

❺ Melt the remaining chocolate chips in the microwave (*ew!*) or using a double boiler (*yay!*). Flip half the cookies over and spread a thin layer of the melted chocolate on the flat side of the flipped cookies.

❻ Light a candle (ask an adult for help!) and gently toast the marshmallows on sticks. When they're good and gooey, put them on the not-chocolated cookies and then squish them together with the chocolated cookies to make a s'more sandwich.

INGREDIENTS

¾ cup (90 grams)	**all-purpose flour**
¾ cup (90 grams)	**whole wheat flour**
2 teaspoons	**ground cinnamon**
1 teaspoon	**baking soda**
Pinch of	**kosher salt**
½ cup (1 stick/113 grams)	**butter**, at room temperature
¾ cup (160 grams)	lightly packed **brown sugar**
2 tablespoons (25 grams)	**granulated sugar**
1	**large egg**
1	**egg yolk**
1 teaspoon	**pure vanilla extract**
2⅔ cups (450 grams)	**dark chocolate chips**
24	**big marshmallows**

LINZER
• COOKIES •

INGREDIENTS

¾ cup (1½ sticks/170 grams)	**butter**, at room temperature
½ cup (100 grams)	**granulated sugar**
Pinch of	**kosher salt**
	Zest of 1 **lemon**
1	**egg yolk**
1 teaspoon	**almond extract**
¾ cup (75 grams)	**almond flour**
1⅓ cups (160 grams)	**all-purpose flour**
	seedless raspberry jam, for filling
	powdered sugar, for dusting

Fun fact: the Linzer torte is the oldest cake ever to be named after a place (in this case, Linz, Austria)—there is a published recipe for Linzer torte from 1696! These cookies are an adaptation of the original Linzer torte—just cookie size! They're traditionally eaten around Christmastime in Germany, Austria, and Switzerland. Baking is great; some things are new and crazy and exciting, and some things are traditions that go back hundreds or even thousands of years.

1 In the bowl of a stand mixer fitted with the paddle attachment or in a large bowl using a hand mixer, cream the butter, granulated sugar, salt, and lemon zest. Scrape the bowl and add the egg yolk and almond extract. Mix well. Scrape the bowl again, add the almond flour, and mix until combined. Scrape one more time and add the all-purpose flour. Beat until combined. Divide the dough in half and form each half into a disc. Wrap the discs in plastic wrap and chill in the fridge for an hour.

2 Preheat the oven to 350°F. Line a couple of sheet pans with parchment paper.

3 On a floured surface, roll each dough disc out to about ⅛ inch thick. Using a 2-inch fluted cutter, cut out cookies and place them on the prepared pans. They can be close together; these cookies don't spread much. Put the pans in the freezer for 15 minutes. With a smaller cookie cutter, cut the centers out of half the cookies.

4 Bake for 12 to 14 minutes, or until they just start to turn golden brown on the edges. Remove from the oven and cool completely on a wire rack.

5 Dust the cookies with the holes with powdered sugar. Spread a thin layer of jam on each of the cookies that don't have a hole in them. Carefully place a sugar-dusted cookie top on each jammed cookie.

MAKES 8
ICE CREAM
SANDWICHES

No-Churn Classic
ICE CREAM SANDWICHES

Dude, these are so amazing. This recipe may look daunting, but you can totally do it. My favorite part is rolling the ice cream sandwiches in sprinkles at the end. You can also just use this recipe to make no-churn ice cream if you don't feel like making cookies.

MAKE THE ICE CREAM

1 Cut two pieces of parchment paper that are 8 inches wide and about 12 inches long and use them to line two 8-inch square cake pans. The ends should stick out above each pan on two sides when you put the parchment in the pan—you'll use those as handles to remove the ice cream from the pan once it's frozen. They make it easy to take the ice cream out without messing up its shape.

2 In a large bowl, whisk together the condensed milk, vanilla, and salt.

3 In the bowl of a stand mixer fitted with the whisk attachment or in a large bowl using a hand mixer, whip the cream until it forms soft peaks. Don't whip it so it's super stiff—that'll make your life miserable later. Fold a scoop of whipped cream into the milk mixture. Now pour the milk mixture into the bowl with the whipped cream and gently fold them together. Pour half of the mixture into one prepared pan and half into the other. Freeze overnight. Put a clean sheet pan in the freezer to chill overnight, too.

MAKE THE COOKIES

4 Preheat the oven to 350°F. Line two sheet pans with parchment paper.

5 In the bowl of a stand mixer fitted with the paddle attachment or in a large bowl using a hand mixer, cream the butter, both sugars, and the salt. Add the egg, egg yolk, and vanilla and beat until fluffy. Whisk the flour and baking soda together and add to the butter mixture. Gently beat until almost combined. Add the chocolate chips and fold by hand to finish combining the dough and distribute the chocolate chips.

INGREDIENTS

FOR THE ICE CREAM

1 (14-ounce/(397-gram) can	**sweetened condensed milk**
2 teaspoons	**pure vanilla extract**
Pinch of	**kosher salt**
2 cups (480 grams)	**heavy cream**

FOR THE COOKIES

10 tablespoons (1¼ sticks/143 grams)	**butter**, at room temperature
¾ cup (150 grams)	lightly packed **brown sugar**
½ cup (100 grams)	**granulated sugar**
Pinch of	**kosher salt**
1	**large egg**
1	**egg yolk**
1 teaspoon	**pure vanilla extract**
1½ cups (180 grams)	**all-purpose flour**
1 teaspoon	**baking soda**
1⅓ cups (226 grams)	**milk chocolate chips**
1⅓ cups (226 grams)	**mini chocolate chips** or **chocolate sprinkles**, for decoration

6 Scoop about 1 tablespoon of the dough and roll it into a small ball in your hand. Place it on one of the prepared pans and gently press down, making a fat burger patty. Repeat with the remaining dough, setting them each about 2 inches apart. Bake for 14 to 16 minutes, or until the edges start to turn brown but the middle is still a bit underdone. Remove from the oven and cool on a wire rack.

7 To assemble the ice cream sandwiches, line a sheet pan with parchment and turn half the cookies upside down on the pan. Find a round cutter that is slightly smaller than your cookies. Fill a bowl with your sprinkles or chocolate chips. Remove the block of ice cream from the container using your handy-dandy parchment handles and place it on the frozen sheet pan. Cut out ice cream circles and place one on each upside-down cookie. Put another cookie on top and roll the edges in the sprinkles to coat. Put in the freezer right away, freeze for a half hour, and then enjoy.

the HISTORY OF COOKIES

Everybody has a cookie. Every culture has some form of sweet little flat cake that they make for treats or holidays, or as an easy-traveling snack. In America, we call 'em cookies (which comes from the Dutch word *koekje*, which means "little cake"). In England and Australia, they're called biscuits. In Germany, they say *keks*. In Spain, they're *galletas*. They're known as *kuki* or *keke* in most of Africa. In Latin, they're *crustulum*. So where do cookies come from and who invented them?

The first-known cookies were baked in Persia in the seventh century. Back then, Persians were renowned for their sweets. They developed incredible cakes and pastries. Their ovens were usually hot stone or clay boxes heated with burning wood. There weren't thermometers, so bakers would test to see how hot the oven was by putting a little cake batter on the stone. These little test cakes became the first cookies!

It didn't take long for the use of sugar to spread to the Mediterranean and then to Northern Europe. And with it came cookies. By the end of the Middle Ages, you could buy cookies in London and Paris. During the Renaissance, cookbooks were being written and many of them had cookie recipes. Also around this time, people were sailing all over the world. These trips lasted for months, and one of the foods sailors ate while out at sea were tough biscuits called hardtack, which could be stored for months or even years without going bad. When these sailors got to America, they brought hardtack with them and also jumbles, sweet little hard biscuits.

In the 1700s, the first cookbook published in the United States had two recipes for cookies. The first cookies in the US were from English, Scottish, and Dutch bakers. Later, during the Industrial Revolution, businesses began mass-producing cookies—along with many other products. Companies like Hetfield & Ducker and VanDerveer & Holmes were producing millions of cookies a year, including the first animal crackers!

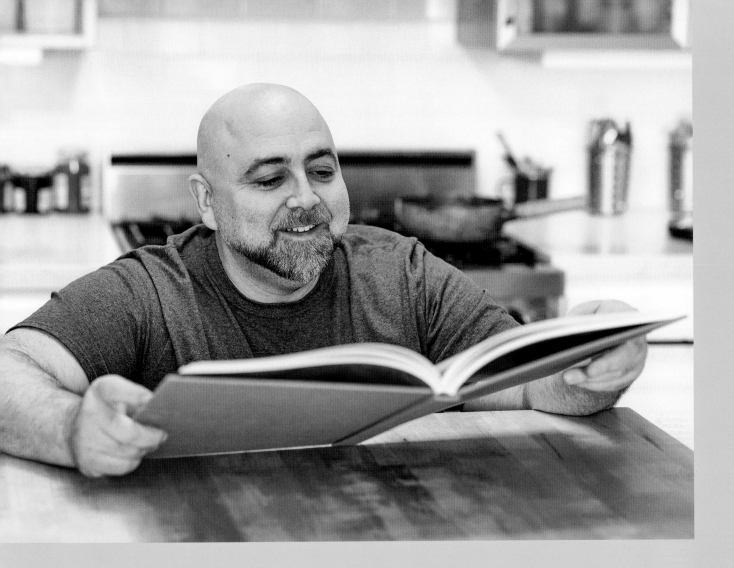

In 1937, something wonderful happened. A woman named Ruth Graves Wakefield, who had a restaurant in Whitman, Massachusetts, called the Toll House, was baking some cookies called "butter drop do." The recipe called for unsweetened baking chocolate, which she didn't have on hand—but she did have some semisweet chocolate. She chopped it up, stirred it into the cookie dough, and chocolate chip cookies were born. In 1997, sixty years after the cookies were invented, they became the official state cookie of Massachusetts.

Other cookies were also invented around this time. In 1891, a guy in Philadelphia, Pennsylvania, named Charles M. Roser invented the Fig Newton. Around 1915, a Japanese landscape architect named Makoto Hagiwara invented the fortune cookie, based on a Japanese rice cracker called *tsujiura senbei*. Ladyfingers have been around for a thousand years, but in 1901, Specialty Bakers in Marysville, Pennsylvania, started making them commercially and almost all the ladyfingers available at retail are now made by them.

People have been making cookies for almost two thousand years, maybe longer. Cookies have all kinds of ingredients, lots of different techniques, and many, many different flavors. Just imagine what other kinds of cookies are waiting to be discovered. Maybe *you* will invent the next great cookie!

UNCLAS
COOKIES

SIFIABLE

COOKIES ARE LIKE ANIMALS. There are so many different kinds that some don't fit into any one category. Like the duck-billed platypus. Is it a mammal? Is it a bird? Who knows? But also like the platypus, all cookies are awesome, no matter what you call them.

MAKES 15 COOKIES

SPRITZ
· COOKIES ·

INGREDIENTS

1 teaspoon	**pure vanilla extract**
2	**large eggs**
2 cups (240 grams)	**all-purpose flour**
½ teaspoon	**baking powder**
Pinch of	**kosher salt**
1 cup (2 sticks/226 grams)	**butter**, at room temperature
¾ cup (150 grams)	**granulated sugar**
	food coloring, 3 colors
	sanding sugar, for decorating

Spritz cookies are really fun, and you can get super creative with them. You can make any shape, pattern, and color you want! They're also fun because you get to squeeze them out of a pastry bag, hence the name. Let's get to spritzin'!

1 Preheat the oven to 350°F. Line a sheet pan with parchment paper.

2 In a bowl using a fork, mix the vanilla and eggs. In another bowl using a *different* fork, mix together the flour, baking powder, and salt.

3 In the bowl of a stand mixer fitted with the paddle attachment, cream the butter and granulated sugar until light and fluffy. Add half the egg mixture, mix it real good, scrape the bowl, and then add the flour mixture. Mix on low for a few seconds, then add the rest of the egg mixture. Mix on low, pause to scrape the bowl, and then mix on low again until juuuuust combined.

4 Divide the dough among three bowls: one bowl with a lot of dough, one bowl with less, and one bowl with even less than that. Use the food coloring to tint the dough in each bowl a different color. Put each color of dough into its own piping bag fitted with a medium-large plain tip.

5 Pipe bull's-eyes of dough onto the prepared pans. Use the bag with the least amount of dough for the centers, then use the second least to pipe a ring around that, and the bag with the most dough to pipe a final ring around the outside. Sprinkle with sanding sugar. If the cookies don't pipe evenly, moisten the tip of your finger and gently smooth the dough out. Freeze the cookies for 10 to 15 minutes.

6 Bake the cookies for about 8 minutes. They should be set but not caramelized—you want the color to stand out. Remove from the oven and cool on a wire rack.

7 If you're feeling crazy, make sandwich cookies with the spritz cookies, sandwiching ganache or jam or peanut butter or marshmallow creme between them.

Rainbow
CHECKERBOARD
· COOKIES ·

These cookies are really fun. You make two different colors of cookie dough and then arrange strips of each color to create a checkerboard when you slice them. You know when you ask what you'll ever use geometry for in real life? This is it.

INGREDIENTS

1 cup (2 sticks/226 grams)	**butter**, at room temperature
1 cup (200 grams)	**sugar**
1	**large egg**
1	**egg yolk**
1 teaspoon	**pure vanilla extract**
3 cups (360 grams)	**all-purpose flour**
1½ teaspoons	**baking powder**
Pinch of	**kosher salt**
	food coloring, any 2 colors you want

❶ In the bowl of a stand mixer fitted with the paddle attachment or in a large bowl using a hand mixer, cream the butter and the sugar. Add the egg, egg yolk, and vanilla and beat some more.

❷ In a medium bowl, whisk together the flour, baking powder, and salt. Add the flour mixture to the butter mixture and beat until combined.

❸ Divide the dough in half and use the food coloring to tint each half a different color. Roll the dough into two identical 6-inch-long logs. Flatten each log into a rectangle that measures 2 × 2 × 6 inches. Take your time and get this right. Wrap each rectangle in plastic wrap and refrigerate for an hour.

❹ With a sharp knife, carefully cut one rectangle lengthwise into thirds. Rotate it 90 degrees and cut into thirds again. Put the strips back in the fridge and repeat with the other rectangle.

❺ Build checkerboards with the two colors and then roll into two checkerboarded logs, firmly pressing the strips together. Refrigerate for 30 minutes.

❻ Preheat the oven to 350°F. Line two sheet pans with parchment paper.

❼ Slice the checkerboard logs into ¼-inch-thick pieces, lay them on the prepared pans, and bake for 9 to 10 minutes, or until they're set but not yet golden brown. Remove from the oven and cool on a wire rack.

ANIMAL CRACKERS

These are some of my all-time favorite cookies. When I was a kid, they came in a box that looked like a circus train car with the most impractical red ribbon attached to it as some sort of carrying device. Made zero sense. But I love their style and their delicate, light flavor. They are slightly sweet, not too sweet, and they really do almost have the texture of a cracker more than a cookie.

1 In a medium bowl, whisk together both flours, the baking powder, and the cinnamon.

2 In the bowl of a stand mixer fitted with the paddle attachment or in a large bowl using a hand mixer, cream the butter, sugar, honey, and salt. Add the egg and vanilla and beat to combine. Add the flour mixture to the butter mixture and beat to combine. Divide the dough in half, form each half into a disc, and wrap each disc with plastic wrap. Chill in the fridge for 45 minutes.

3 Preheat the oven to 350°F. Line two sheet pans with parchment paper.

4 Roll out the dough to about ¼ inch thick. Use animal-shaped cutters to cut out different animal shapes and place them on the prepared pans. Freeze for 10 minutes and then bake for about 13 minutes, until they just start to turn golden brown. Remove from the oven and cool on a wire rack.

INGREDIENTS

1 cup (120 grams)	**all-purpose flour**
1 cup (120 grams)	**whole wheat flour**
1 teaspoon	**baking powder**
1 teaspoon	**ground cinnamon**
½ cup (1 stick/113 grams)	**butter**, at room temperature
¼ cup (50 grams)	**granulated sugar**
2 tablespoons (42 grams)	**honey** or **real maple syrup**
Pinch of	**kosher salt**
1	**large egg**
1½ teaspoons	**pure vanilla extract**

MAKES 30 COOKIES

Rainbow
MERINGUE
• COOKIES •

INGREDIENTS

4	**egg whites**
¾ cup (150 grams)	**granulated sugar**
Pinch of	**kosher salt**
Pinch of	**cream of tartar**
1 teaspoon	**pure vanilla extract**, or ½ teaspoon of any other extract you want
	gel food coloring
	sprinkles, for decorating (optional)

Meringue cookies are so magical, so light and ethereal—and to make them even more magical, these cookies are rainbow colored. If there were ever a cookie that could claim the title of "Official Unicorn Poop," these are it. There's no wrong way to color or decorate these cookies, so go to town and have fun.

1 Preheat the oven to 225°F. Line two sheet pans with parchment paper.

2 Put some water in a medium pot and bring it to a simmer. Place the egg whites and sugar in the bowl of a stand mixer. Place the bowl over the simmering water and stir with a wooden spoon until all the sugar dissolves and the mixture is warm to the touch. (This is how you make what's called a Swiss meringue.)

3 Fit the stand mixer with the whisk attachment and place the bowl on the mixer. Starting on medium speed, whip the egg whites until they get frothy. Add the salt, cream of tartar, and vanilla (or other extract). Raise the mixer speed to high and whip until stiff peaks form. Be patient.

4 Fit a piping bag with a large piping tip. Paint different colors of gel food coloring on the inside of the piping bag. Fill the bag with the meringue and pipe out balls or rosettes or whatever shape you want. Optional: Decorate with sprinkles.

5 Bake the meringues for 1 hour 15 minutes, then turn the oven off, leave the door closed, and leave the cookies in there overnight.

6 Store in an airtight container at room temperature.

FORTUNE
· COOKIES ·

⊰ INGREDIENTS ⊱

2	egg whites
1 teaspoon	almond extract
Pinch of	kosher salt
½ cup (60 grams)	all-purpose flour
½ cup (100 grams)	granulated sugar
A few tablespoons	cold water

Half the fun of these cookies is making your own fortunes! These are tricky because you have to fold the cookies while they are still hot, so make sure there is an adult helping you.

❶ Preheat the oven to 400°F. Line two sheet pans with parchment paper. Write out 10 fortunes on small slips of paper.

❷ In a large bowl, whip the egg whites, almond extract, and salt until frothy. In a separate bowl, whisk together the flour and sugar. Fold the flour mixture into the egg white mixture until a paste forms. Add about a tablespoon of cold water at a time until the batter gently self-levels. Spoon the batter onto the prepared pans, two portions per pan, and spread each portion into a 3-inch circle with the back of a spoon.

❸ Bake for 5 to 8 minutes, until the edges turn golden brown. Remove from the oven and, working quickly, place a fortune on a cookie, lift the cookie with an offset spatula, and fold it gently in half to enclose the fortune. Place the flat edge of the cookie on the rim of a heavy coffee mug and fold the cookie backward over the lip of the mug. Repeat to fill and form the warm cookies, placing them in a muffin tin so they hold their shape while they cool. Repeat with the remaining batter.

THE HISTORY OF FORTUNE COOKIES

For me, fortune cookies are one of the best parts about going out for Chinese food in America. They have fun fortunes or sayings inside them—and sometimes when you get a really good one, you stick it in your wallet. But where did fortune cookies come from? They're not Chinese, funnily enough.

In the 1800s in Japan, there was a cookie kinda like a fortune cookie called *omikuji senbei* or *tsujiura senbei*. It had the same shape as fortune cookies do today but was bigger and darker and was made with sesame oil and miso. It came with a fortune, but the fortune was placed in between the horns of the cookie and not on the inside.

Three people claim to have invented the modern fortune cookie: David Jung of the Hong Kong Noodle Company in Los Angeles, Seiichi Kito from Little Tokyo in Los Angeles, and Makoto Hagiwara of the Japanese Tea Garden in San Francisco. Who really invented it first? No one knows. But I think it is fair to say that fortune cookies are definitely an American invention with Asian roots. There is also no Chinese word for "fortune cookie," which I find hilarious.

Rolled
WAFER
• COOKIES •

INGREDIENTS

8 tablespoons (1 stick/113 grams)	**butter**, at room temperature
1 cup (200 grams)	**granulated sugar**
Pinch of	**kosher salt**
4	**egg whites**
½ teaspoon	**almond extract**
¾ cup (90 grams)	**all-purpose flour**
¼ cup (28 grams)	**almond flour**
½ cup (85 grams)	**chocolate chips** (optional)

Okay, these are some of the most exciting cookies you will ever make! You have to pull them out of the oven and pick them up while they're still hot and wrap them around the handle of a wooden spoon. Gotta be tough and get your head in the game for these cookies. It's worth it, though. Biting into a fresh hollow cookie is an amazing experience.

1 Preheat the oven to 400°F. Line two sheet pans with parchment paper.

2 In a large bowl, cream the butter, granulated sugar, and salt using a stand or hand mixer. Add the egg whites and almond extract. Mix well. Add the all-purpose flour and beat until combined.

3 Scoop four 2-tablespoon mounds of dough onto each prepared pan. Sprinkle each with a pinch of almond flour.

4 Bake one pan at a time for 3 to 4 minutes, until the edges of the cookies are golden brown. Working quickly, remove the cookies from the oven and, while they're still warm, roll them around the handle of a wooden spoon to form a tube. Let them cool on a wire rack set over a sheet of parchment.

5 Optional: Melt the chocolate in the microwave (*ew!*) or using a double boiler (*yay!*) and drizzle it onto the cooled cookies.

MANDELBROT

This is a traditional Jewish cookie that my great-grandmother made, so this is how I make it. The recipe uses margarine because in traditional Jewish cooking, you are not supposed to mix milk and meat in the same meal. You can absolutely use regular butter if you want. I like these cookies because they really speak about where my people are from. Eastern European Jews in the early 1900s didn't have fancy refrigerators and plastic wrap. These cookies were great because they never really go stale. I mean, they do, but you can't tell because they're a pretty dry cookie to begin with. That doesn't make them sound delicious, but I promise they are.

INGREDIENTS

2 cups (264 grams)	**all-purpose flour**
½ cup (55 grams)	**almond flour**
½ cup (85 grams)	**potato starch**
2 teaspoons	**ground cinnamon**
Pinch of	**kosher salt**
¾ cup (1½ sticks/170 grams)	**nondairy margarine**, at room temperature
1¼ cups (250 grams)	**granulated sugar**
	Zest of 1 **navel orange**
3	**large eggs**
1 teaspoon	**pure vanilla extract**
¾ cup (98 grams)	**slivered almonds**, roughly chopped
¾ cup (127 grams)	**dark chocolate chips**

❶ In a medium bowl, whisk together the all-purpose flour, almond flour, potato starch, 1 teaspoon of the cinnamon, and the salt.

❷ In a large bowl, cream the butter, 1 cup (200 grams) of the sugar, and the orange zest using a stand or hand mixer. Add the eggs and vanilla and mix until smooth. Add the flour mixture to the butter mixture and stir to combine. Add the almonds and chocolate chips and stir them in by hand. Divide the dough in half, wrap each half in plastic wrap, and refrigerate for 30 minutes.

❸ Shape each portion of dough into a log about 9 inches long and 2 inches wide and place on parchment paper on a sheet pan. Refrigerate for another 30 minutes.

❹ Preheat the oven to 350°F.

❺ Bake the logs on the sheet pan for 40 minutes, or until they just begin to brown. Let cool for 1 hour. (You can turn off the oven while the logs cool—just remember to preheat it again if you do.) With a serrated knife, cut each log into ½-inch-thick segments. In a small bowl, combine the remaining ¼ cup (50 grams) sugar and 1 teaspoon cinnamon. Dip the cut sides of each segment into the cinnamon sugar and return them to the sheet pan, cut-side up. Bake for 12 minutes, then flip the pieces and bake for another 12 minutes, or until they begin to turn golden brown. Remove from the oven and cool on a wire rack.

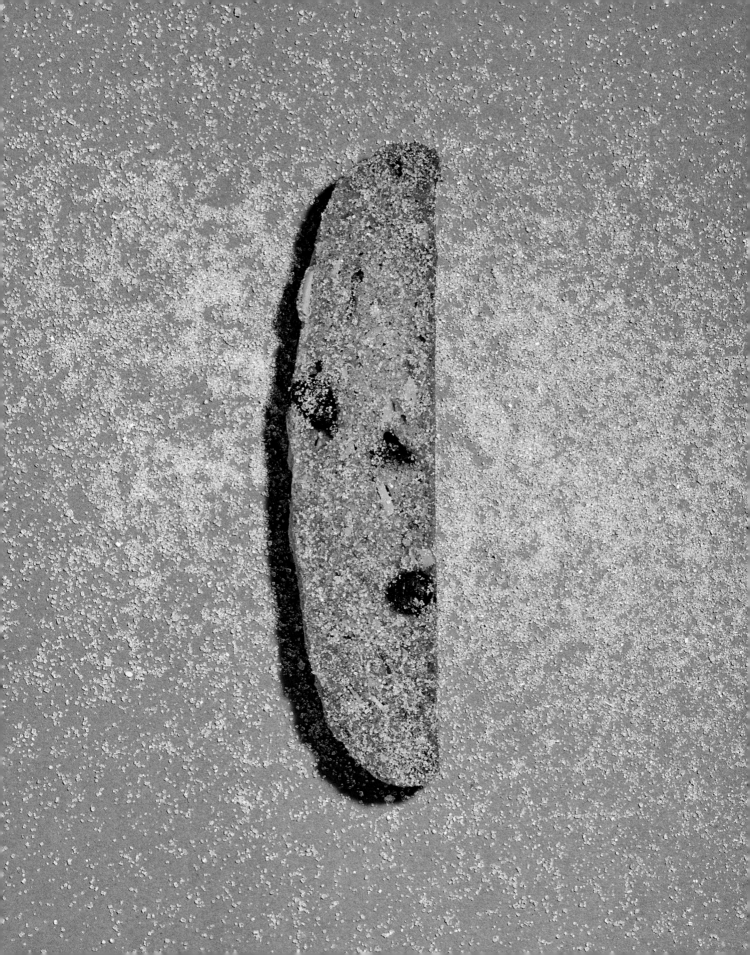

MILK-&-COOKIE

Moments

One of the things I love about food—besides cooking it, eating it, tasting it, talking about it, and dreaming about it—is the ceremony of it. The rituals of food are one of the aspects of a meal that we all look forward to. Here are some of my favorite food rituals.

1. Dunking warm cookies into a cold glass of milk is one of the most beautiful, pure moments you can have. When the milk floods into all the little holes in the cookie and everything gets cold and crispy just for a second, it is perfection.

2. Getting fortune cookies after a big meal of Chinese food and reading them aloud to the whole table. Confession: sometimes I trade fortunes under the table because I like someone else's better.

3. Going to a baseball game and getting a giant cardboard tray of hot dogs *and* nachos *and* soft pretzels covered in mustard *and* roasted-in-the-shell peanuts *and* popcorn *and* frozen lemonade *and* Dippin' Dots *and* one more hot dog.

4. The first spoonful from a new jar of creamy peanut butter.

5. The corner bite of a sandwich.

6. Pouring syrup on a stack of pancakes at a diner while on a road trip.

7. Licking your fingers after eating an entire rack of BBQ ribs.

8. When you're pouring your own fountain soda and you time it just right and stop at the exact moment where you're getting the most soda for the price but you can still get the lid on without spilling any.

9. Drinking out of a coconut.

10. Forgetting you have a candy bar in your pocket so it melts into a liquid and when you discover it, you open one end of the package and squeeze the liquid candy bar into your mouth like you're eating toothpaste from the tube.

11. Getting some junk food at the drive-through and eating your fries while driving because they're hot and eating them later makes no sense.

12. Drinking the Dorito crumbs straight from the bag after you've eaten all the whole chips.

13. Eating leftovers at, like, three a.m., especially Chinese food, pizza, pot roast, pasta, cold hamburgers, 24-hour-old coffee drinks, and birthday cake that's already been cut into.

DECOR

COOKIES

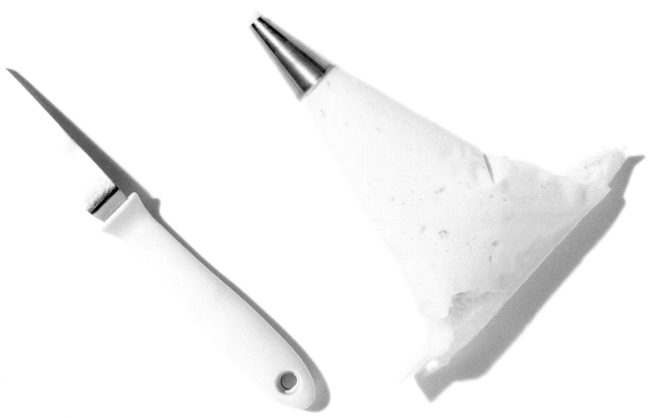

SOME COOKIES AREN'T JUST BAKED, cooled, and eaten. Sometimes, they get decorated. A lot! Look online and you'll find some really, really amazing decorated cookies. I find it always helps me to draw a picture of what I want to make first. That way, I can look at the picture and figure out what different techniques I want to use to make it a reality. There's stiff royal icing for piping, thin royal icing for flooding, food coloring for painting, and about a billion different kinds of sprinkles and candies to use. You can totally let your imagination go wild, but a little planning will help you create your dream cookie.

SUGAR
• COOKIES •

These are a good, solid, easy sugar cookie recipe. You can also bake them as much or as little as you want. They can be really pale and soft, or you can bake them so they're golden brown and crispy. These are also perfect for decorating with royal icing (there are recipes on page 127).

1 In a medium bowl, whisk together the flour, baking powder, and salt.

2 In a large bowl, cream the butter and sugar using a stand or hand mixer. Add the egg, vanilla, and almond extract. Beat until light and smooth. Add the flour mixture to the butter mixture and beat until combined.

3 Divide the dough in half and place each half on a piece of parchment paper. Roll out the dough to ¼ inch thick. Cover with another sheet of parchment paper and place on a sheet pan. Chill in the fridge for 30 minutes.

4 Preheat the oven to 350°F. Line two sheet pans with parchment paper.

5 Cut out cookies from the chilled dough. (Sugar cookies can be just about any shape you want!) Place the shapes on the prepared pans and freeze for 15 minutes.

6 Bake for 10 to 12 minutes, or until the cookies are just barely golden brown on the edges. Remove from the oven and cool on a wire rack before eating or decorating.

INGREDIENTS

2¼ cups (280 grams)	**all-purpose flour**
1 teaspoon	**baking powder**
Pinch of	**kosher salt**
¾ cup (1½ sticks/170 grams)	**butter**, at room temperature
¾ cup (150 grams)	**granulated sugar**
1	**large egg**
1 teaspoon	**pure vanilla extract**
1 teaspoon	**almond extract**

Royal Icing

I have a few different recipes for royal icing. Sometimes, I want the icing to be loose so I can flood the top of a cookie. Sometimes, I want it stiff for piping decorations. Some recipes use meringue powder and some use fresh egg whites. I like using the meringue powder recipe best because it can be rewhipped after a day, but I don't always have meringue powder on hand, so sometimes I just use old-school egg whites. All these recipes are super easy to color with food coloring. You can also flavor these with vanilla, cinnamon, or any other spice you want. Just remember that if you add cinnamon or another dark spice, you'll see it. Also, it's best to make royal icing just before you plan to use it. It works best when it's fresh.

Royal Icing (with Meringue Powder)

FOR FLOODING

Makes 2 cups

3 tablespoons (25 grams)	**meringue powder**
Pinch of	**kosher salt**
4 cups (480 grams)	**powdered sugar**, sifted, plus more if needed
½ cup (120 grams)	**water**, plus more if needed

Put the meringue powder, salt, and powdered sugar in a bowl and whisk together. Add all the water and whisk until the mixture is smooth. Adjust the consistency with more water or more powdered sugar. Store the icing in an airtight container with a damp paper towel touching the surface or directly in a plastic piping bag.

Royal Icing (with Meringue Powder)

FOR PIPING

Makes 2 cups

¼ cup (33 grams)	**meringue powder**
Pinch of	**kosher salt**
4 cups (480 grams)	**powdered sugar**, sifted
6 tablespoons (90 grams)	**water**

Put the meringue powder, salt, and powdered sugar in a bowl and whisk together. Add the water and whip vigorously. If the icing is too thick, add a bit more water drop by drop and whisk on high speed using an electric mixer. The icing will get fluffy and stiff and should be bright white. Store the icing in an airtight container with a damp paper towel touching the surface or directly in a plastic piping bag.

Royal Icing (with Egg Whites)

FOR FLOODING

Makes 2 cups

3	**egg whites**
Pinch of	**cream of tartar**, or 1 teaspoon **distilled white vinegar** or **fresh lemon juice**
4 cups (480 grams)	**powdered sugar**
Pinch of	**kosher salt**

In a medium bowl, whip the egg whites until foamy. Add the rest of the ingredients and whip until smooth and white. If the icing is too thick to pour, add a few drops of water at a time until it's the right consistency. Store the icing in an airtight container with a damp paper towel touching the surface or directly in a plastic piping bag.

Royal Icing (with Egg Whites)

FOR PIPING

Makes 2 cups

3	**egg whites**
4½ cups (540 grams)	**powdered sugar**
Pinch of	**kosher salt**
Pinch of	**cream of tartar**, or 1 teaspoon **distilled white vinegar** or **fresh lemon juice**

In a medium bowl, whip the egg whites until foamy. Add the rest of the ingredients and whip until stiff and bright white. If the icing is too thick to whip, add a few drops of water at a time until it moves more easily. Store the icing in an airtight container with a damp paper towel touching the surface or directly in a plastic piping bag.

Royal Icing Directions

Remember to store your royal icing in an airtight container. If it dries out, hard crunchy bits will get stuck in your piping bag and make you miserable. Lay a damp paper towel on the surface of the royal icing when you are not actively putting it in a piping bag. If you get crunchy bits, *do not* try to stir them back in the rest of the icing. It won't work. Trust me. Carefully spoon them out and toss.

TO MAKE A PAPER CONE (OR "CORNET") FOR PIPING:

① Take a piece of parchment paper and cut it diagonally from corner to corner.

② Pick up the triangle and, with the 90-degree angle pointing down, put the side with the short arm of the triangle in your right hand.

③ Fold the corner in your right hand over toward yourself to make a cone with the point facing up.

④ Roll the cone all the way up, then flip it so the point is facing down.

⑤ Adjust the cone so the point is sharp and closed, then fold down the corner sticking up to hold the bag in place.

⑥ Fold the open end of the cone closed and fill it halfway full with icing.

⑦ Cut the tip off to make a hole as big or as small as you want.

⑧ Squeeze with your thumb and start piping!

PRO TIPS: Don't use waxed paper—it's literally the worst. In a pinch, you can use regular printer paper, but it's pretty stiff. Parchment paper is really the best way to go. And don't use the piping bag like a pencil—the tip should not touch the cookie. Instead, lay your royal icing down like it's a rope.

Piping Royal Icing

First select the tip you want to use and place the tip on your piping bag or cornet, then fill with the icing.

To pipe a solid border, give the bag a tiny squeeze so just a centimeter of icing comes out. Touch the icing to the cookie and begin squeezing with light, even pressure. As the icing comes out, move the bag to direct where the icing will go. Remember, keep the tip at least a centimeter above the cookie so the icing comes out and gently lies on the surface of the cookie. It's not a pencil.

To pipe rosettes or dots, place the piping bag about 3 millimeters above the cookie. Start squeezing gently while holding the bag completely still. If you want to make a bubble, allow the pressure from the bag to inflate the bubble. The bubble will grow naturally. If you move your hand, you'll get a bullet shape. When the bubble is the size you want, stop squeezing altogether and give the bag a quick twist to separate the bubble from the icing left in the bag. This takes practice, but once you get it down, you can do hundreds of bubbles in a minute.

For a shell border, it's the same as piping bubbles, except you are using a star tip, and instead of holding the bag perpendicular to the cookie, you hold it at an angle. Again, hold the bag totally still to let the shell form, then pull the icing as you release the pressure.

For rosettes, start with the tip a few millimeters above the surface of the cookie and gently twirl the bag as you pipe. To separate the rosette from the icing left in the bag, give a quick twist or flip of the bag. Again, this takes practice.

PRO TIP: For all these techniques, it helps if you make a steady noise with your mouth as you pipe. For bubbles, I say "bloop," for rosettes, I say "werrrrmp," and for shells, I make a fart sound. It's funny, but it works.

Flooding with Royal Icing

Flooding is when you want to cover the surface of a cookie with a smooth, flat layer of icing. You can flood a cookie with one color or several. If you want more than one color, make sure you make all the colors of icing you want *before* you start piping. Royal icing dries fast, so for a perfectly smooth layer, all the different colors have to be liquid.

To flood with one solid color, make your royal icing, color it, and then pipe the boundary of where you want the icing to stop. Once the border is piped, begin filling the inside of the shape you piped. Be careful not to overfill the cookie. If there are bald spots, use a toothpick to kinda spread the icing around so you don't pipe too much.

If you want a different color for the border, use a thicker royal icing and pipe the border. Allow it to set up for 10 minutes and then flood the inside.

To make hearts, flood the cookie in one color, then pipe dots in a different color. Allow the dots to settle into the flood and then drag a toothpick through the dots to form heart shapes.

Painting on Royal Icing

Painting on cookies is really fun and makes them very special. To start, first flood your cookie. You can do any color, but I find that white makes the best cookie canvas. Allow the icing to dry completely—overnight is best. Next, select the colors you want to use. Gel colors work best. Squeeze out a little color onto a coffee can lid or a plate. You can use the gel straight out of the bottle, or thin it out with a few drops of water to give it a watercolor effect, or (this is very advanced) mix the gel color with a powder called titanium dioxide, which will make the gel behave like acrylic paint. Use real (clean) paintbrushes, but if you don't have any, you can use a cotton swab. They're not as accurate, but they get the job done.

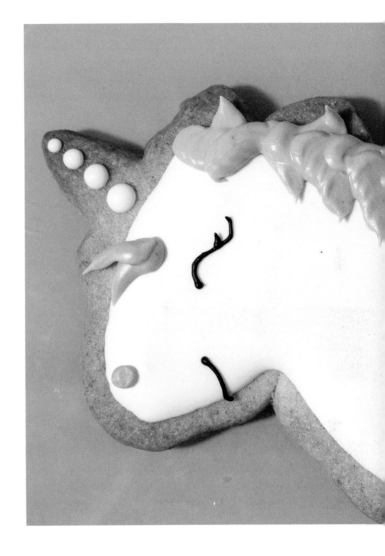

MAKES 1
DOUBLE-LAYER
COOKIE CAKE

Giant
COOKIE
CAKE

I used to always see these giant cookie cakes at the cookie stand in the mall, and I always wanted one. I never got one, so I became a pastry chef and figured out how to make my own. You'll need some pizza pans to make these, but they're easy to find. Make sure not to bake these too long. If they are too crispy, they are hard to slice.

❶ Preheat the oven to 350°F. Lightly grease with butter two 10-inch pizza pans.

❷ In a medium bowl, whisk together the flour, cornstarch, baking soda, and salt.

❸ In a large bowl, cream the butter and both sugars using a stand or hand mixer. Add the eggs and vanilla and beat until smooth. Add the flour mixture to the butter mixture and beat to combine. Add the chocolate chips and fold them in by hand.

❹ Divide the dough in half and spread each half evenly over the prepared pizza pans. Bake for 23 to 25 minutes, until the edges start to turn brown. Remove from the oven and cool completely on a wire rack.

❺ When the cookies are cool, spread the marshmallow creme over one cookie and place the other cookie on top. Decorate any way you like, then slice like a cake and enjoy!

⟩ INGREDIENTS ⟨

	butter, to grease the pans
4 cups (500 grams)	**all-purpose flour**
1½ tablespoons (12 grams)	**cornstarch**
2 teaspoons	**baking soda**
Pinch of	**kosher salt**
1½ cups (3 sticks/340 grams)	**butter**, at room temperature
1½ cups (300 grams)	lightly packed **brown sugar**
½ cup (100 grams)	**granulated sugar**
2	**large eggs**
1½ tablespoons (20 grams)	**pure vanilla extract**
2 cups (380 grams)	**chocolate chips**
1 (7½-ounce/213-gram) jar	**marshmallow creme**

COOKIE-CRUMB CRUSTS

We need ingredients to make cookies, but what happens when the cookies *are* the ingredients?

Cookies make great ingredients for other delicious things, and one of the most versatile of those is the cookie-crumb crust. You can make all kinds of desserts with cookie-crumb crusts. Basically, you take a bunch of dry cookies (gotta be dry—chewy cookies turn to mush) and pulse them in a food processor to make crumbs, add butter and sugar, and press the mixture into a baking dish or pie plate. Sometimes you bake the crust by itself and fill it after it cools, sometimes you bake the crust and the filling together, and sometimes you don't need to bake it at all. Here are a few ideas for different kinds of cookie crusts.

1. Graham cracker crusts: Graham crackers are delicious, and in addition to being used in cookie crumb crusts, they are also a very important part of one of the most delicious and iconic desserts of all time . . . s'mores! You can use graham cracker crusts for:

- New York cheesecake
- Key lime pie
- Peanut butter pie
- S'mores pie
- Lemon bars
- Banana cream pie

2. Oreo crusts: These are crusts made with the most delicious cookies ever made—Oreos. They're super chocolaty and don't need much extra sugar. Some great desserts with Oreo crusts are:

- Chocolate cream pie
- Cookies-and-cream cheesecake
- No-bake pumpkin cheesecake
- Chocolate cheesecake
- Snickers pie
- Chocolate peanut butter pie

3. Those are the two cookies that you'll see most often for crusts, but there are lots of other cookies you can use, such as:

- Nilla wafers
- Biscoff cookies
- Famous Amos chocolate chip cookies
- Nutter Butters
- Dry, crunchy oatmeal cookies

Honestly, you can use almost any cookie as long as it is dry and will crumble. My advice? Get creative! Adding a cookie to any crust almost automatically makes it better.

THINGS
WITH
COOKIES
IN

THEM

SOMETIMES DELICIOUS COOKIES AREN'T THEMSELVES the goal of baking delicious cookies. Sometimes cookies are an ingredient used to make something else even more amazing. Cookies as an ingredient can offer different flavors and textures to things that would otherwise be a little plain. Pudding and whipped cream are delicious and all, but add cookies? Now we're talking.

MAKES 20 BROWNIES

COOKIE BROWNIES

INGREDIENTS

Nonstick baking spray

FOR THE BROWNIE BATTER

½ cup and 2 tablespoons (75 grams)	**all-purpose flour**
½ cup (50 grams)	**unsweetened cocoa powder**
1 teaspoon	**baking soda**
¾ cup (1½ sticks/170 grams)	**butter**, at room temperature
1 cup (200 grams)	**granulated sugar**
⅓ cup (71 grams)	lightly packed **brown sugar**
Pinch of	**kosher salt**
2	**large eggs**
1 teaspoon	**pure vanilla extract**
½ cup (85 grams)	**chocolate chips**

FOR THE COOKIE DOUGH

1¼ cups (150 grams)	**all-purpose flour**
1 teaspoon	**baking soda**
½ cup (1 stick/113 grams)	**butter**, at room temperature
¾ cup (160 grams)	lightly packed **brown sugar**
¼ cup (50 grams)	**granulated sugar**
Pinch of	**kosher salt**
1	**large egg**
1 teaspoon	**pure vanilla extract**
1 cup (170 grams)	**chocolate chips**

TO FINISH

1 cup (170 grams)	**white chocolate chips**

I love brownies. I love cookies. This recipe is perfect for me. It's fun to mix these two recipes and get them to bake together juuuuuust right. I wonder what other combinations I can come up with . . .

1 Preheat the oven to 350°F. Lightly spray a 9 × 13 casserole pan with nonstick baking spray.

MAKE THE BROWNIE BATTER:

2 In a medium bowl, mix the flour, cocoa powder, and baking soda.

3 In a large bowl, cream the butter, both sugars, and the salt using a stand or hand mixer. Add the eggs and vanilla and beat until smooth. Add the flour mixture to the butter mixture and mix. Add the chocolate chips and fold them in by hand to combine. Scrape the brownie batter evenly into the prepared casserole pan.

MAKE THE COOKIE DOUGH

4 In a medium bowl, whisk together the flour and baking soda.

5 In a large bowl, cream the butter, both sugars, and the salt using a stand or hand mixer. Add the egg and vanilla and beat until smooth. Add the flour mixture to the butter mixture and beat to combine. Fold in the chocolate chips by hand.

6 Drop chunks of the cookie dough into the brownie batter. Make sure some chunks of dough touch the bottom with some brownie batter on top. Bake for 25 minutes, or until the edges start setting up. Sprinkle the white chocolate chips on top and bake for 5 to 6 more minutes. Remove from the oven and cool for an hour, then cover and chill in the fridge for 2 to 3 hours. Slice and eat this bad boy cold.

MAKES 1 PIE

Peanut Butter
COOKIE
PIE

I got this idea from my friend Rodney Henry. He plays a mean guitar and bakes the best pies. He has a recipe for a very special pie called "The Baltimore Bomb" that has these cookies from Baltimore in it called Berger Cookies. It's my favorite pie that he makes. This pie is kinda like that but instead of the Bergers, it uses one of my favorite cookies: Nutter Butters! They are peanut buttery and sweet and salty, and this pie really is . . . the bomb.

MAKE THE CRUST

1 Preheat the oven to 350°F.

2 Put the cookies, sugar, and salt in the bowl of a food processor and pulse until the mixture has the texture of sand. Transfer to a bowl and stir in the melted butter to combine really well. Dump into a 9-inch pie plate and press down until the crumb mixture is in a firm, even layer. Bake for 8 minutes. Set aside on a wire rack to cool.

MAKE THE FILLING

3 In a large bowl, beat the cream cheese so it is soft and pliable. Scrape the bowl and add the condensed milk, vanilla, and salt. Beat until smooth. Add the lemon juice and beat until smooth. Fold in the chopped cookies by hand.

4 Pour the filling into the cooled piecrust. Sprinkle the chocolate chips and sprinkles (if you want) evenly over the pie and refrigerate for 6 hours before serving.

INGREDIENTS

FOR THE PIECRUST

26	**Nutter Butter cookies**
¼ cup (50 grams)	**granulated sugar**
Pinch of	**kosher salt**
6 tablespoons (¾ stick/85 grams)	**butter**, melted

FOR THE FILLING

1 (8-ounce/226-gram) package	**cream cheese**, cold
1 (14-ounce/396-gram) can	**sweetened condensed milk**
1 teaspoon	**pure vanilla extract**
Pinch of	**kosher salt**
⅓ cup (80 grams)	**fresh lemon juice** (from about 2 **lemons**)
10	**Nutter Butter cookies**, roughly chopped

FOR THE TOPPING

¾ cup (127 grams)	**milk chocolate chips**
¼ cup (40 grams)	**chocolate sprinkles** (optional)

SERVES 8 TO
10 PEOPLE

Cookie SALAD

Okay, my friend Molly Yeh first introduced me to cookie salad on the set of *Spring Baking Championship.* I was a little skeptical. Cookie salad?! What craziness is that? Then she made some for me, and I was hooked. Cookie salad is as delicious as it is ridiculous.

MAKE THE PUDDING

1 In a bowl, whisk together the flour, granulated sugar, salt, egg yolks, and cream. Pour into a medium saucepot and heat over medium heat, stirring, until the mixture thickens. If you stop stirring and one bubble boils up from the bottom, take the pudding off the heat. You are done. Pour the pudding into a bowl, stir in the butter and vanilla, and press a piece of plastic wrap directly against the surface of the pudding. Cool at room temperature for at least 90 minutes.

MAKE THE COOKIES

2 In a large bowl, cream the butter, powdered sugar, vanilla, and salt using a stand or hand mixer. Add the flour and mix to combine. Add the chocolate chips and stir them in by hand. Divide the dough in half, wrap each half in plastic wrap, and refrigerate for 30 minutes.

3 Preheat the oven to 350°F. Line a sheet pan with parchment paper.

4 Roll out the dough and cut it into shapes. (A doughnut shape is traditional, but you do you. I like making cookies in animal shapes.) Place the cookies on the prepared pan and bake for about 12 minutes, or until they start browning on the edges. Remove from the oven and cool on a wire rack.

5 Optional: Melt the chocolate in the microwave (*ew!*) or using a double boiler (*yay!*), transfer it to a piping bag, and pipe designs onto your cooled cookies. Let it set for 5 minutes.

INGREDIENTS

FOR THE PUDDING

3 tablespoons (24 grams)	**all-purpose flour**
6 tablespoons (75 grams)	**granulated sugar**
Pinch of	**kosher salt**
3	**egg yolks**
1½ cups (360 grams)	**heavy cream**
1 tablespoon (14 grams)	**butter**
1 teaspoon	**pure vanilla extract**

FOR THE COOKIES

½ cup (1 stick/(113 grams)	**unsalted butter**, at room temperature
½ cup (60 grams)	**powdered sugar**
1 teaspoon	**pure vanilla extract**
Pinch of	**kosher salt**
1 cup (130 grams)	**all-purpose flour**
14 tablespoons (150 grams)	**dark chocolate chips** (optional)

TO ASSEMBLE

2 (11-ounce/312-gram) cans	**mandarin orange slices**
1½ cups (360 grams)	**heavy cream**
¼ cup (30 grams)	**powdered sugar**
	sprinkles and **chocolate chips** (optional)

6 To assemble the salad, open the cans of oranges and drain them really well. Set about 15 orange slices aside for decoration. Put like two-thirds of the cookies in a plastic bag and crush them into big chunks. In a large bowl, whip the cream and powdered sugar to stiff peaks. Fold the pudding into the whipped cream. Next, fold the crushed cookies into the whipped cream/pudding mixture, then fold in the oranges. Pour this "salad" into a serving bowl and decorate the top with the whole cookies and the orange slices that you saved. Refrigerate until ready to serve.

7 To serve, remove from the fridge and sprinkle with some sprinkles and chocolate chips (if you want). Thanks, Molly!

MAKES 1 QUART ICE CREAM

• NO-CHURN •
Cookies 'n' Cream
ICE CREAM

INGREDIENTS

FOR THE COOKIES

1 cup (120 grams)	**all-purpose flour**
¾ cup (75 grams)	**unsweetened cocoa powder**
½ teaspoon	**baking soda**
½ cup (1 stick/113 grams)	**butter**, at room temperature
½ cup (100 grams)	**granulated sugar**
Pinch of	**kosher salt**
1	**large egg**

FOR THE ICE CREAM

1 (14-ounce/396-gram) can	**sweetened condensed milk**
2 teaspoons	**pure vanilla extract**
Pinch of	**kosher salt**
2 cups (480 grams)	**heavy cream**

This ice cream is super easy to make and is seriously some of the best ice cream I have ever had. A kid from *Kids Baking Championship* introduced it to me. I'll never buy an ice cream machine again. This is a recipe for cookies 'n' cream, but you can use any cookie you want, or you can omit the cookies and just make any ol' ice cream you can think of.

❶ Put a quart container in the freezer. Preheat the oven to 325°F.

MAKE THE COOKIES

❷ In a medium bowl, mix the flour, cocoa powder, and baking soda.

❸ In a large bowl, cream the butter, sugar, and salt using a stand or hand mixer. Add the egg and beat to combine. Add the flour mixture to the butter mixture and beat until combined. Press the dough flat, wrap it in plastic wrap, and refrigerate for 15 minutes.

❹ Roll the dough out on a sheet of parchment paper, then set the dough (on the parchment) on a sheet pan and bake for 15 to 18 minutes, or until the dough is baked through to the center. Remove from the oven and cool on a wire rack. It's totally cool if this giant cookie breaks into pieces when you take it off the pan. When the cookie/cookie pieces are cool, smash them up in a plastic bag and pour them back on a piece of parchment paper to dry them out.

MAKE THE ICE CREAM

❺ In a medium bowl, stir together the condensed milk, vanilla, and salt. In a large bowl, whip the cream to firm peaks. Add a dollop of the whipped cream to the condensed milk mixture and fold together, then pour the condensed milk mixture into the bowl with the whipped cream and gently fold until almost combined. Add the cookie crumbs and fold until combined but not so much that the cookie crumbs and cream start melting into each other.

❻ Remove the frozen quart container from the freezer, dump the whipped cream mixture in there, and freeze for at least 5 hours before serving.

CHAPTER
9

THINGS
THAT ARE **SORTA**

COOKIES

I LIKE TO CALL THESE THINGS "COOKIE ADJACENT."
They resemble cookies or have cookielike properties,
but they're just not quite "cookies." Maybe they're
more like cake but they look like a cookie. Or maybe
they have all the same ingredients as a cookie but
they're squishier. They're all great, but they're not
exactly cookies. They're just *sorta* cookies.

MAKES 1 QUART

Edible

COOKIE DOUGH

If you have ever made chocolate chip cookies, you know the best part is licking the beater after the cookies go in the oven. Fresh cookies are great, but raw cookie dough is where it's at, and unlike dough made with raw eggs, this one is totally safe to eat. This recipe is also great as an ice cream mix-in. Try it with the ice cream recipe on page 145.

1 This is weird, but put your flour into a microwave-safe bowl and heat it in the microwave for 1 minute. This will keep you from getting a tummy ache from eating raw flour. Remove it from the microwave and let it cool.

2 In a large bowl, cream the butter, both sugars, the vanilla, and the salt using a stand or hand mixer. Beat in the cooled flour until combined. Adjust the consistency with the milk—you may not need to use it all—while keeping in mind that the dough will get stiffer in the fridge. Add the toasted walnuts, chocolate chips, and sprinkles and stir them in by hand. Keep the dough refrigerated in an airtight container until you're ready to eat it.

INGREDIENTS

2 cups (240 grams)	**all-purpose flour**
1 cup (2 sticks/226 grams)	**butter**
1 cup (213 grams)	lightly packed **brown sugar**
¼ cup (50 grams)	**granulated sugar**
2 teaspoons	**pure vanilla extract**
Pinch of	**kosher salt**
2 tablespoons (30 grams)	**whole milk**
¾ cup (98 grams)	**walnuts**, toasted
¾ cup (128 grams)	**chocolate chips**
¼ cup (40 grams)	**sprinkles**

MAKES 1 QUART

COOKIE BUTTER

INGREDIENTS

FOR THE COOKIES

2 cups (240 grams)	**all-purpose flour**
2 teaspoons	**baking soda**
1½ teaspoons	**ground ginger**
1 teaspoon	**ground cinnamon**
Big pinch of	**kosher salt**
1 cup (200 grams)	**granulated sugar**, plus more for rolling
¾ cup (164 grams)	**canola oil**
¼ cup (70 grams)	**molasses**
1	**large egg**

FOR THE COOKIE BUTTER

2 tablespoons (28 grams)	**butter**, at room temperature
½ teaspoon	**pure vanilla extract**
Pinch of	**ground cinnamon**
Pinch of	**ground nutmeg**
Pinch of	**ground cloves**
Pinch of	**ground ginger**
Pinch of	**kosher salt**
¼ cup (60 grams)	**whole milk**

Okay. Think peanut butter, but instead of ground-up peanuts, it's ground-up cookies. I know, right?

MAKE THE COOKIES

❶ Preheat the oven to 350°F. Line a sheet pan with parchment paper.

❷ In a bowl, whisk together the flour, baking soda, ginger, cinnamon, and salt.

❸ In a large bowl, cream the sugar, oil, and molasses using a stand or hand mixer. Add the eggs one at a time and beat until combined. Add the flour mixture to the sugar mixture and beat to combine. Scrape the bowl during the process and try not to overmix.

❹ Place some sugar in a bowl. Roll the dough into 1-inch balls, roll each ball in the sugar to coat, and place them on the prepared pan. Bake for 10 to 12 minutes, rotating the pan halfway through so the cookies bake evenly. It's really important not to overbake these so the middles stay mushy. Remove from the oven and immediately remove the parchment from the pan and set it on the counter so the cookies stop baking. After 2 minutes, transfer the cookies from the parchment to a wire rack to cool completely.

MAKE THE COOKIE BUTTER

❺ Grind up the cookies in the bowl of a food processor to make superfine crumbs. Add the butter, vanilla, cinnamon, nutmeg, cloves, ginger, and salt and buzz, buzz, buzz.

❻ Slowly drizzle in the milk, pulsing the food processor until you like the consistency. Store your cookie butter in an airtight container in the fridge.

BLACK and WHITE

• COOKIES •

It wasn't until later in life that I discovered the joys of perfect black and white cookies. And by "perfect," I mean a little stale, with a nice solid crust on the icing that crackles when you bite it and thin edges just slightly overbaked so there's a ring of more solid cookie around the softer cakey cookie in the middle. The best part about these cookies? They're huge.

MAKE THE COOKIES

1 Preheat the oven to 350°F. Line two sheet pans with parchment paper.

2 In a medium bowl, whisk together the flour, baking powder, baking soda, and salt.

3 In the bowl of a stand mixer fitted with the paddle attachment or in a large bowl using a hand mixer, cream the butter and granulated sugar. Scrape the bowl, add the egg, and beat to combine. Scrape the bowl again and add the lemon zest; beat to combine. Add the flour mixture and mix for a few seconds to get it started, then scrape the bowl. Add the sour cream, scrape the sides, and mix for a few seconds. Finish mixing with a wooden spoon or rubber spatula.

4 Drop about ¼-cup portions of the batter onto the prepared pans. They'll spread, so make sure there is plenty of room between each plop; you can probably fit 6 cookies per sheet pan. Bake for 15 to 18 minutes, rotating the pans and swapping the one on the bottom rack and the one on the top rack once during baking so the cookies bake evenly. The edges of the cookies should juuuuuust start to brown. Don't overbake the cookies or they'll be gross. Let the cookies cool for a few minutes on the pans, then transfer them to a wire rack to cool completely. If you don't cool them on a rack, they can steam themselves and get gummy. Gummy is for bears, not cookies.

MAKE THE ICING

5 In a medium bowl, whisk together the powdered sugar, corn syrup, vanilla, salt, and 6 tablespoons (90 grams) of the milk. Divide the mixture evenly between two bowls. Add the cocoa powder to one bowl and whisk to combine. Adjust the consistency of the chocolate icing with the remaining 2 tablespoons (30 grams) of milk so it is the same as the white frosting.

INGREDIENTS

FOR THE COOKIES

1¾ cups (219 grams)	**all-purpose flour**
½ teaspoon	**baking powder**
½ teaspoon	**baking soda**
Big pinch of	**kosher salt**
10 tablespoons (1¼ sticks/148 grams)	**butter**, at room temperature
1 cup (200 grams)	**granulated sugar**
1	**large egg**
Pinch of	**lemon zest**
⅓ cup (80 grams)	**sour cream**

FOR THE ICING

5½ cups (640 grams)	**10x powdered sugar**
2 tablespoons (35 grams)	**corn syrup**
1 teaspoon	**pure vanilla extract**
Pinch of	**salt**
½ cup (120 grams)	**whole milk**
3 tablespoons plus 1 teaspoon (24 grams)	**unsweetened cocoa powder**

152   Things That Are Sorta Cookies

6 Spread the chocolate icing over half of the flat side of each cookie and set them icing-side up on a sheet pan. Put the cookies in the fridge for 5 minutes, then coat the other half of the flat side with white icing and let it set.

7 Enjoy these cookies as they were meant to be—with a Dr. Brown's black cherry soda and a pastrami on rye with mustard.

N'awlins PRALINES

INGREDIENTS

1 cup (210 grams)	**granulated sugar**
1 cup (225 grams)	lightly packed **light brown sugar**
¾ cup (180 grams)	**heavy cream**
4 tablespoons (½ stick/56 grams)	**butter**, at room temperature
½ teaspoon	**baking soda**
2¼ cups (212 grams)	**pecan halves**
1 teaspoon	**pure vanilla extract**
Pinch of	**kosher salt**

MY FAVORITE THINGS IN NEW ORLEANS

- Boiled crawfish
- Beignets
- Eggs Benedict
- Bananas Foster
- Chargrilled oysters
- Smoked sausage
- Boudin
- Bánh mì
- Po'boy sandwiches
- Muffuletta sandwiches
- King Cake with a little plastic baby hidden inside
- Pralines
- Chicory coffee
- Tabasco
- Gelato and cannolis at Angelo Brocato's

In cooking, it seems that the word "praline" can refer to almost any combination of nuts and sugar, but there are some specific kinds of pralines, too. There are softer-centered confections from Belgium called pralines that you can usually find in chocolate box samplers, and there is another European praline that is a little firmer. The American praline comes from New Orleans, where emancipated African American bakers added cream to the European recipes and substituted pecans for almonds, creating the classic praline that we have in this country. It's more like fudge than a cookie. You also don't bake it in the oven. You cook the dough on the stovetop and let the cookies cool to room temperature. Always have an adult with you when you're making these cookies, as they can be dangerous to make. Hot sugar hurts.

1 Line two sheet pans with parchment paper. Find your 1-tablespoon cookie scoop. Attach a candy thermometer to the side of a medium pot. Get all your ingredients together, because once you start this process, you can't stop to measure something or go to the store to get something you don't have!

2 Put both sugars, the cream, butter, and baking soda in the pot. Bring to a slow boil over medium-high heat, stirring nonstop with a wooden spoon. Watch the thermometer. When it reaches exactly 236°F, remove the pot from the heat and place it on a heat-safe surface that won't scorch.

3 Immediately add the pecans and stir with a wooden spoon for EXACTLY 3 minutes. Add the vanilla and salt and stir for another 30 seconds.

4 Working quickly, use the cookie scoop to scoop up the praline mixture and plop portions on the prepared pans. If the mixture gets too firm because you're slow, the good news is you can heat it back up so it flows again. Allow the pralines to cool at room temperature (if you put them in the fridge to cool, they get weird and gross). Store in an airtight container at room temperature.

MAKES 24 CONES

Ice Cream
CONES

Okay, you need a waffle-cone iron for this. It looks like a regular waffle iron, but it's much thinner and it comes with a cone mold to roll your ice cream cones on. You might not have one, but that's okay—you can also make these in a nonstick pan on the stovetop over a relatively low flame. The nice thing about stovetop waffles is you don't have to roll these—you can also use a small bowl as a mold instead to make waffle cups. Just drop the warm waffle directly on top of the bowl and stuff it in there.

❶ In a medium bowl, whisk together the flour, sugar, and salt. Add the eggs and milk and whisk to combine. While whisking, slowly drizzle in the melted butter. Let the batter sit at room temperature for 30 minutes.

❷ Set the waffle-cone iron to heat level 6. When it's hot, pour a spoonful or two of the batter onto the iron and cook for 2 to 3 minutes. Using an offset spatula, quickly lift the cone off the iron and wrap it around the cone mold. Set the cone inside a tall drinking glass to cool so it holds its shape and repeat with the remaining batter.

INGREDIENTS

1⅓ cups (160 grams)	**cake flour**
½ cup (100 grams)	**granulated sugar**
Pinch of	**kosher salt**
2	**large eggs**
¼ cup (60 grams)	**whole milk**
4 tablespoons (½ stick/56 grams)	**butter**, melted

MAKES 24 GRAHAM CRACKERS

GRAHAM CRACKERS

The funny thing about graham crackers is that they were invented by some health food guy to calm people down. They were intentionally boring, made from just water and whole wheat flour. Everyone was like, "Yeah, no," so they added cinnamon and sugar and ginger and nutmeg and honey and then everyone was like, "Dope." Make these graham crackers, then try making your own marshmallows, too, and use them together for the best s'mores you will ever eat in your entire life.

1 In a medium bowl, whisk together the egg, oil, honey, half the milk, and the vanilla.

2 In a large bowl, whisk together the whole wheat flour, all-purpose flour, sugar, baking powder, cinnamon, nutmeg, ginger, and salt. Make a well in the center of the flour mixture and pour the egg mixture in. Stir with a fork to combine. If the dough seems too stiff, drizzle in a bit more milk. Turn the dough out onto the counter and gently knead until it comes together. Divide the dough in half, wrap each half in plastic wrap, and chill in the fridge for an hour.

3 Preheat the oven to 300°F. Line a sheet pan with parchment paper.

4 Roll out each half of the dough until it's really thin, about ⅛ inch thick. Place it on the prepared pan and brush lightly with the remaining milk. Sprinkle with the cinnamon sugar. Use a pizza cutter to cut the dough into squares—don't separate them, just cut the lines. Prick the squares with a fork to keep them from bubbling as they bake.

5 Bake the cookies for 10 minutes, then check them. If the lines you cut have disappeared, cut them again. If not, rotate the pan and bake for another 15 minutes, or until the graham crackers start to brown. Turn off the oven and crack open the oven door. Let the graham crackers sit in the oven for 20 to 25 minutes, then remove from the oven and cool on a wire rack.

INGREDIENTS

1	**large egg**
¼ cup (50 grams)	**vegetable oil**
¼ cup (80 grams)	**honey**
¼ cup (60 grams)	**whole milk**, plus more if needed
1 teaspoon	**pure vanilla extract**
1 cup (113 grams)	**whole wheat flour**
1 cup (120 grams)	**all-purpose flour**
¼ cup (50 grams)	**granulated sugar**
1 teaspoon	**baking powder**
1 teaspoon	**ground cinnamon**
Pinch of	**ground nutmeg**
Pinch of	**ground ginger**
Pinch of	**kosher salt**
¼ cup (50 grams)	equal parts **cinnamon** and **sugar**, mixed

See photos pages 160–161

The two main sweeteners that you'll be using *most* of the time are brown sugar and white (aka granulated) sugar. I say "most of the time" because there are lots of other sweeteners out there, like corn syrup, honey, and coconut sugar and all the sugar replacers like monk fruit and stevia and whatnot.

Brown sugar and white sugar come from sugarcane and sugar beets. These are two agricultural products that have a high sugar content. After being harvested, sugarcane and sugar beets are refined and turned into pure granulated white sugar and several by-products. One of those by-products is molasses. Molasses is added back to white sugar to create brown sugar. When less molasses is added to the sugar, it becomes *light* brown sugar; and when more is added, it becomes *dark* brown sugar.

Brown sugar and white sugar have different properties that make them good for different recipes. For instance, chocolate chip cookies that only have white sugar in them are flatter and crispier because white sugar doesn't have any moisture in it. When it melts in the oven and then cools, it gets super crispy. A lollipop is just melted sugar—if you think about a lollipop mixed with butter and flour and chocolate chips, it kinda gives you an idea of how white sugar works.

On the other hand, chocolate chip cookies that have only brown sugar in them tend to be fatter and chewier. The next time you use brown sugar, stick your finger in it and rub your fingers together. The brown sugar is a little sticky from all the molasses. The molasses adds moisture to the sugar, so when it melts in the oven, it doesn't dry super crisp like white sugar. Also, the molasses is acidic, so when you mix baking powder with brown sugar, it creates a chemical reaction that produces carbon dioxide, and this makes the cookies rise and get soft and thick. Another thing I like about brown sugar is that it tastes really good. Molasses has an earthy and complex taste, which, in my opinion, makes for a much more interesting chocolate chip cookie.

When I make chocolate chip cookies, I like them to be thin and crispy. But I also like the flavor of brown sugar, so I use both white and brown sugar. The brown sugar makes the cookies chewier in the middle where the cookie is thick and makes it taste delicious. The white sugar makes the edges of the cookies crispier where they are thinner. Find the right combination of brown sugar and white sugar, and you can make *your* perfect chocolate chip cookie, too.

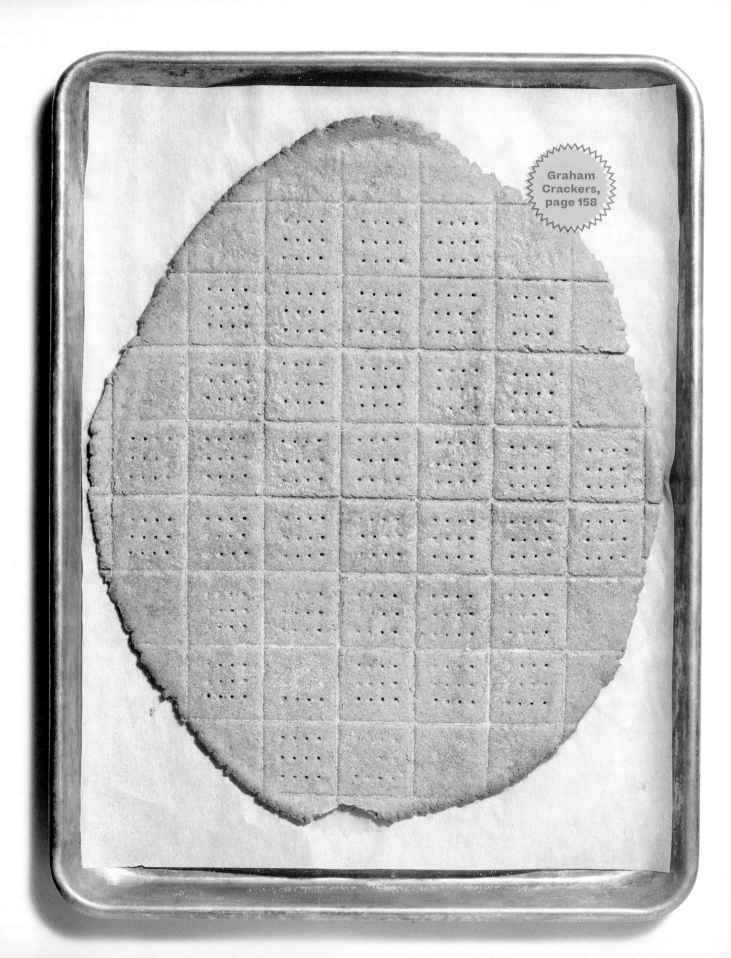

Graham Crackers, page 158

HOLIDAY COOKIES

HOLIDAYS ARE GREAT! You get to see family. Celebrate. Reconnect with your people. But let's not kid ourselves. Holiday season is *cookie* season! So many of our celebrations would feel incomplete without the cookies that go with them. Would Purim be Purim without hamantaschen? Would Christmas be Christmas without gingerbread? Our cookies define our festivals, so let's make some good ones and celebrate!

Chocolate CRINKLE

• COOKIES •

INGREDIENTS

1 cup (125 grams)	**all-purpose flour**
½ cup (50 grams)	**unsweetened cocoa powder**
1 teaspoon	**baking soda**
Big pinch of	**kosher salt**
½ cup (1 stick/115 grams)	**butter**, at room temperature
½ cup (100 grams), plus 1 cup (200 grams)	**granulated sugar**, for rolling
½ cup (100 grams)	lightly packed **dark brown sugar**
1	**large egg**
1 teaspoon	**pure vanilla extract**
1 cup (150 grams)	**semisweet chocolate chips**
1 cup (130 grams)	**powdered sugar**, for rolling

I like to think of these cookies as the best parts of a brownie, in the correct ratio. A tiny super-thin crust of sugary chocolate encapsulates a gooey, almost raw brownie batter. Plus, when you roll them in powdered sugar and then bake them, they get all these awesome cracks. How cool is that?

❶ In a medium bowl, whisk together the flour, cocoa powder, baking soda, and salt.

❷ In the bowl of a stand mixer fitted with the paddle attachment, cream the butter, ½ cup (100 grams) of the granulated sugar, the brown sugar, egg, and vanilla. Slowly add the flour mixture to the butter mixture in three stages. Using a wooden spoon, fold in the chocolate chips. This dough is supposed to be thick and sticky. Chill in the fridge for an hour.

❸ Preheat the oven to 350°F. Line two sheet pans with parchment paper.

❹ Put the remaining 1 cup (200 grams) granulated sugar in a bowl and the powdered sugar in another. Scoop roughly 1½-tablespoon portions of dough and roll them into balls. Coat each ball lightly in granulated sugar, then heavily in powdered sugar. This helps keep the powdered sugar stuck to the cookie without making it translucent. Place the cookies on the prepared pans, leaving at least 3 inches between each cookie.

❺ Bake for 12 minutes. Remove from the oven and let cool on a wire rack. DO NOT OVERBAKE. These cookies are a work of art when done right and very mediocre when overbaked.

GINGERBREAD
Pine Cones

INGREDIENTS

¾ cup (170 grams)	**butter**, at room temperature
⅔ cup (136 grams)	lightly packed **light brown sugar**
½ cup (140 grams)	**corn syrup**
¼ cup (75 grams)	**molasses**
Pinch of	**kosher salt**
1 tablespoon (5 grams)	**ground ginger**
1 teaspoon	**ground cinnamon**
1 teaspoon	**ground nutmeg**
½ teaspoon	**ground cloves**
3½ cups (420 grams)	**all-purpose flour**
	powdered sugar, for dusting

This is a really good, solid gingerbread recipe. I was in a baking store and I saw this really cool cookie mold shaped like a pine cone and I knew I had to have it. I thought this would be a perfect gingerbread cookie and if I could make it look like it got snowed on, that would be awesome.

❶ In a bowl, cream the butter, brown sugar, corn syrup, and molasses. Add the salt and spices and cream until smooth. Add the flour; beat to combine. Divide the dough in half and press it flat. Wrap in plastic wrap and refrigerate for 1 hour.

❷ Preheat the oven to 350°F and cover two sheet pans with parchment paper. Flour the table and roll the cookie dough to ½ inch thick. Press the cookie mold onto the dough really hard to get an impression. Lift the mold off and cut the pine cone out. Carefully place it on a sheet pan and repeat. Bake for 9 to 12 minutes. Cool on a wire rack.

❸ When the cookies are cool, stand them almost upright and sift powdered sugar over them so the parts of the cookie that stick out catch the powdered sugar. Cool, right?

MAKES 36 COOKIES

CANDY CANE

• SUGAR COOKIES •

INGREDIENTS

1 cup (2 sticks/227 grams)	**butter**, at room temperature
1 cup (200 grams)	**granulated sugar**
1½ teaspoons	**peppermint extract**
1 teaspoon	**baking powder**
Pinch of	**kosher salt**
1	**large egg**
2¾ cups (385 grams)	**all-purpose flour**
	red food coloring
1	**egg white**
2 tablespoons (25 grams)	**sanding sugar**, for decoration

These cookies are really fun to make, and the cool thing is that you can make any colors you want and any flavors you want. You can do yellow-and-orange lemon-flavored cookies for summer. You can do purple-and-blue coffee-flavored cookies for autumn. You can do cinnamon-flavored rainbow cookies for spring. You can make anything you want!

1 In the bowl of a stand mixer fitted with the paddle attachment or in a large bowl using a hand mixer, cream the butter, granulated sugar, peppermint extract, baking powder, salt, and egg until smooth. Add the flour and beat to combine. Divide the dough in half. Put half the dough back in the mixer bowl and wrap the other half in plastic wrap. Add red food coloring to the dough in the mixer bowl until you like the color. Remove the dough from the bowl and wrap it in plastic wrap. Refrigerate both colors of dough for 90 minutes.

2 Preheat the oven to 350°F. Line your sheet pans with parchment paper.

3 Roll the red dough into an 18-inch-long log and cut it into 36 pieces. Roll each piece into a snake that is 5 inches long. Repeat with the white dough. Twist one red snake and one white snake together to make a spiral, place on a prepared pan, and curve the top to look like a candy cane. When you have filled the pans, freeze the cookies for 10 minutes.

4 Brush each cookie lightly with the egg white and sprinkle with the sanding sugar. Bake for 8 to 10 minutes, or until you see the slightest bit of brown on the edges. Remove from the oven and cool on a wire rack. Store at room temperature.

Date & Walnut
RUGELACH

Ooooo, these are fancy. I love dates. They're one of my favorite foods. There's a Persian market near my house and they have the juiciest, sweetest dates I've ever had. Rugelach is a Jewish cookie that we eat at lots of different holidays, and it may be the first cookie I ever tasted.

MAKE THE DOUGH

1 Combine all the ingredients for the dough in the bowl of a food processor. Pulse until a dough forms. Turn it out onto the counter and divide it in half. Form each half into a disc and wrap in plastic wrap. Chill in the fridge for 90 minutes.

MAKE THE FILLING

2 Place all the filling ingredients in the bowl of a food processor and pulse until you have a not-quite-smooth paste. Set aside.

3 Preheat the oven to 350°F. Line a sheet pan with parchment paper.

4 Roll out one disc of dough into a round that's ⅛ inch thick and about 10 inches across. Spread half the filling over the dough. Cut the round into 12 wedges (like pizza slices) with a pizza cutter. Roll each slice up starting at the wide end. Place them point-side down on the prepared pan. Repeat with the other disc of dough and remaining filling. Brush each cookie with egg wash and sprinkle with turbinado sugar, or regular white sugar if that's all you have.

5 Bake for 25 to 28 minutes, or until the cookies are golden brown. Remove from the oven and cool on a wire rack. Store at room temperature.

INGREDIENTS

FOR THE DOUGH

1¼ cups (174 grams)	**all-purpose flour**
Big pinch of	**kosher salt**
½ cup (1 stick/113 grams)	cold **butter**
½ (8-ounce/226-gram) package	**cream cheese**, cold
1	**egg yolk**

FOR THE FILLING

¼ cup (53 grams)	lightly packed **brown sugar**
2 tablespoons (25 grams)	**granulated sugar**
½ cup (65 grams)	**walnut pieces**, lightly toasted
¼ cup (65 grams)	**soft pitted dates**
2 teaspoons	**ground cinnamon**
Pinch of	**kosher salt**
1	**egg**, for egg wash
	turbinado sugar, for sprinkling

HAMANTASCHEN

Hamantaschen are cookies that were traditionally eaten during the Jewish festival of Purim but are increasingly enjoyed all year long. Haman was an enemy of the Jewish people a long time ago, and we celebrate his defeat by eating cookies that look like his three-cornered hat. I know, sounds weird, but it's saner than an egg-laying bunny. The poppy seed filling is the way to go, but I've given you a couple other traditional filling options, too.

INGREDIENTS

FOR THE POPPY SEED FILLING

1 cup (240 grams)	**whole milk**
½ cup (100 grams)	**granulated sugar**
	zest of 1 **orange**
1 cup (142 grams)	**poppy seeds**
⅓ cup (80 grams)	**dark raisins**
	juice of 1 **lemon**
1 tablespoon (14 grams)	**butter**
2 teaspoons	**pure vanilla extract**

FOR THE DOUGH

1 cup (130 grams)	**powdered sugar**
2	**egg yolks**
½ cup (1 stick/113 grams)	**butter**, at room temperature
	zest of 1 **lemon**
2¼ cups (270 grams)	**all-purpose flour**
Pinch of	**kosher salt**
1	**egg**, for egg wash

MAKE THE POPPY SEED FILLING

1 Put the milk, granulated sugar, orange zest, poppy seeds, and raisins in a medium pot. Bring to a simmer over medium heat and cook, stirring frequently, for about 15 minutes. The mixture should get nice and thick. Add the lemon juice, butter, and vanilla. Stir to combine. Remove from the heat, cover, and let cool.

MAKE THE DOUGH

2 Put the powdered sugar and egg yolks in the bowl of a food processor and pulse to combine. Add the butter and lemon zest and pulse to make a paste. Add the flour and salt a bit at a time and pulse until the dough comes together. Divide the dough in half and form each portion into a disc. Wrap each disc in plastic wrap and refrigerate for at least an hour.

3 Preheat the oven to 350°F. Line two sheet pans with parchment paper.

4 Roll out one disc of dough to ¼ inch thick and cut it into 3-inch rounds. Place the rounds 1 inch apart on one of the prepared pans and place the pan in the fridge for 20 minutes. Repeat with the other disc of dough.

5 Put a heaping teaspoon of filling on each dough round and then press up the sides to form a three-sided pyramid shape. Brush some egg wash on each cookie and bake for 15 to 17 minutes, or until the cookies begin to turn golden brown. Remove from the oven and cool on a wire rack.

Filling Variations

PRUNE FILLING

2½ cups (400 grams)	**pitted prunes**
1 cup (240 grams)	**water**
½ cup (120 grams)	**orange slices**
1 teaspoon	**orange zest**
Pinch of	**kosher salt**
½ cup (107 grams)	lightly packed **brown sugar**
½ teaspoon	**almond extract**

1 Put everything in a pot except for the brown sugar and the almond extract. Stir it up and bring to a boil over medium-high heat. Reduce the heat to maintain a simmer, cover, and cook for 20 minutes. Make sure you check on it and give it a stir once in a while. Don't let the prunes burn.

2 Remove the lid and simmer for 4 to 5 more minutes to let the water evaporate. When there is just a little bit of water left in the pot, remove from the heat and stir in the brown sugar. Keep stirring until all the sugar dissolves. Allow the mixture to cool for 30 minutes, then pour it into the bowl of a food processor (careful—it's still hot) and pulse until smooth. Add the almond extract and pulse a little more. Put the filling in an airtight container and refrigerate overnight before using.

CHOCOLATE FILLING

3 tablespoons (42 grams)	**butter**
⅓ cup (57 grams)	**dark chocolate chips**
¼ cup (50 grams)	**granulated sugar**
1 teaspoon	**pure vanilla extract**
Pinch of	**kosher salt**
1	**large egg**
2 teaspoons	**cornstarch**

1 Melt the butter and chocolate using a double boiler. When they have mostly melted, take the bowl off the saucepan and whisk until completely melted and smooth. Add the sugar, vanilla, and salt and whisk. It won't be super smooth, but that's okay. Let it cool, uncovered, for about 20 minutes.

2 When it has cooled off, add the egg and cornstarch and whisk again until smooth. Chill in the fridge for 15–20 minutes before using.

Fun Things for

DECORATING

There are millions of different kinds of sprinkles and candies you can use to decorate your cookies. Here are just a few.

Semi-sweet chocolate chips

Nuts

Coconut

Sprinkles

Food coloring

- M&M's
- Chocolate sprinkles
- Colored sprinkles
- Dragées—so many beautiful ones, including pearls, silver, and even gold
- Sanding sugar
- Molded sprinkles—stars, hearts, snowflakes . . . there are so many!
- Sixlets—bright colored candy outside and chocolate on the inside
- Sprinkle mixes—some premixed sprinkles are really beautiful
- Edible glitter
- Nonpareils
- Mini chocolate chips
- Mini peanut butter cups
- Coconut flakes
- Powdered sugar
- Cocoa powder
- Peppermints
- Butter mints
- Chocolate drops
- Gumdrops

Sanding sugar

Dragées

Milk chocolate chips

Edible glitter

Ramadan

DATE

• COOKIES •

These cookies use semolina flour, which is a type of flour made from durum wheat. It is a little more coarse than traditional wheat flour and gives these cookies a terrific and unique texture. The method for these cookies is similar to mooncakes. You make a dough, and then fill it and press it into a mold. You can get a traditional ma'amoul cookie mold, but you can also use a mini-muffin tin or just shape them by hand.

MAKE THE DOUGH

1 In a large bowl, mix the semolina flour, all-purpose flour, sugar, and yeast. Add the butter and orange blossom water and work the mixture until it comes together and forms a ball. Cover with a damp kitchen towel and let the dough sit for 90 minutes.

MAKE THE FILLING

2 Put the dates, butter, and cinnamon in the bowl of a food processor and pulse until a smooth paste forms. Divide the paste into 40 portions and form each into a disc about 1½ inches across. Cover with plastic wrap and refrigerate until needed.

3 Preheat the oven to 400°F. Line a sheet pan with parchment paper.

4 Cut the dough into about 40 pieces and cover with plastic wrap. With your hands, press one piece of dough into a 3-inch disc (keep the others covered). Lay a disc of filling in the center and fold the edges of the dough over it. Press the filled dough into a ma'amoul mold, then tap it out. Place the cookie on the prepared pan and repeat with the remaining dough and filling.

5 Bake for 15 to 18 minutes, until golden brown. Remove from the oven and cool on a wire rack.

⟩ INGREDIENTS ⟨

FOR THE DOUGH

2 cups (350 grams)	**semolina flour**
5 tablespoons (50 grams)	**all-purpose flour**
¼ cup (50 grams)	**granulated sugar**
¼ teaspoon	**instant yeast**
10 tablespoons (1¼ sticks/131 grams)	**butter**, at room temperature
3 tablespoons (45 grams)	**orangeblossomwater**

FOR THE FILLING

12 ounces (340 grams)	**dates**, pitted
2 tablespoons (28 grams)	**butter**, at room temperature
1 teaspoon	**ground cinnamon**

MAKES 36 COOKIES

PSL

· COOKIES ·

My wife, Johnna, looooves pumpkin spice lattes. Every year she gets so excited when she gets to go to the coffee shop for her first PSL of the season. I made this recipe for her so she could have that pumpkin spice and coffee flavor whenever she wants.

MAKE THE COOKIES

1 Preheat the oven to 375°F. Line two sheet pans with parchment paper.

2 In a medium bowl, whisk together the flour, espresso powder, baking soda, ginger, cinnamon, cloves, nutmeg, cardamom, and salt.

3 In a large bowl, cream the shortening, granulated sugar, pumpkin, molasses, and egg using a stand or hand mixer. Add the flour mixture to the shortening mixture and beat until smooth.

4 Place some granulated sugar in a bowl. For each cookie, scoop a 1-tablespoon portion of the dough into your hand and roll it into a ball, then roll it in the sugar to coat. Place the cookies on the prepared pans about 2 inches apart. Bake for 7 to 8 minutes; they should look underbaked. Remove from the oven and cool on a wire rack set over a sheet of parchment paper.

MAKE THE GLAZE

5 Whisk together all the glaze ingredients. Adjust with more water or more powdered sugar to thin or thicken the glaze. Drizzle the glaze on the cooled cookies. Store at room temperature to let it set.

INGREDIENTS

FOR THE COOKIES

2¼ cups (270 grams)	**all-purpose flour**
1 tablespoon	**instant espresso powder**
2 teaspoons	**baking soda**
Pinch of	**ground ginger**
Pinch of	**ground cinnamon**
Pinch of	**ground cloves**
Pinch of	**ground nutmeg**
Pinch of	**ground cardamom**
Pinch of	**kosher salt**
½ cup (56 grams)	**vegetable shortening**
1 cup (200 grams)	**granulated sugar**, plus more for rolling
¼ cup (60 grams)	**pure pumpkin puree**
2 tablespoons (40 grams)	**molasses**
1	**large egg**

FOR THE GLAZE

2 cups (260 grams)	**powdered sugar**, plus more if needed
2 tablespoons (30 grams)	**warm water**, plus more if needed
1 tablespoon	**instant espresso powder**
Pinch of	**ground cinnamon**
Pinch of	**kosher salt**

MAKES 24 COOKIES

PECAN TASSIES

These are the perfect dessert for me. I love pecan pie, but sometimes I don't want a whole piece. Pecan tassies are like little mini pecan pies with shortbread for the crust. Y'all, listen. When you get maple syrup, get real maple syrup. From Vermont. In an aluminum can. The stuff that comes in a plastic person-shaped bottle is *not* maple syrup. If you've never had the real thing, you're in for a treat.

MAKE THE DOUGH

1 In the bowl of a food processor, grind the pecans into fine crumbs. Add the butter and cream cheese and pulse to combine. Add the flour and pulse to combine. Turn the dough out onto the counter, then gently knead by hand. Wrap in plastic wrap and refrigerate for 1 hour.

2 Preheat the oven to 350°F. Spray a 24-cup mini-muffin pan with nonstick spray. Scoop 1 tablespoon of the dough into each cup. Press the dough evenly up the sides. Place the muffin tin in the freezer while the oven heats.

MAKE THE FILLING

3 In a medium bowl, whisk together the brown sugar, maple syrup, egg, vanilla, and salt.

4 Remove the muffin tin from the freezer. Put a teaspoon of the chopped pecans into each cup, then fill almost to the top with the filling. Bake for 20 to 25 minutes, or until the pastry is golden brown. Remove from the oven and let cool completely in the pan.

INGREDIENTS

FOR THE DOUGH

½ cup (65 grams)	**pecans**, lightly toasted
½ cup (1 stick/113 grams)	**butter**, at room temperature
½ (8-ounce/113-gram) package	**cream cheese**, at room temperature
1 cup (120 grams)	**all-purpose flour**

FOR THE FILLING

⅔ cup (142 grams)	lightly packed **brown sugar**
2 tablespoons (40 grams)	**real maple syrup**
1	**large egg**
2 teaspoons	**pure vanilla extract**
Pinch of	**kosher salt**
½ cup (65 grams)	chopped **pecans**, lightly toasted

MAKES 36 COOKIES

Cape Cod
CRANBERRY
· COOKIES ·

In Sandwich, Massachusetts, where I grew up, we grew cranberries. Once a year the cranberries would ripen, turn pink, and then all the Ocean Spray trucks would roll into town and get all the cranberries. I love these cookies because no matter where I am when I eat one, I might just be eating a cranberry from my hometown.

INGREDIENTS

1½ cups (180 grams)	**all-purpose flour**
1 teaspoon	**baking soda**
1 teaspoon	**ground cinnamon**
Pinch of	**kosher salt**
1 cup (2 sticks/226 grams)	**butter**, at room temperature
1 cup (220 grams)	lightly packed **brown sugar**
¼ cup (50 grams)	**granulated sugar**
2	**large eggs**
1 teaspoon	**pure vanilla extract**
3 cups (336 grams)	**rolled oats**
1½ cups (170 grams)	**dried unsweetened cranberries**
1 cup (170 grams)	**white chocolate chips**, melted

1 Preheat the oven to 350°F.

2 In a medium bowl, mix together the flour, baking soda, cinnamon, and salt.

3 In a large bowl, cream the butter and both sugars using a stand or hand mixer. Add the eggs one at a time and beat until the mixture is light and fluffy. Add the vanilla and beat some more. Add the flour mixture to the butter mixture and beat to combine. Add the oats and cranberries and mix them in by hand. Cover and let the dough sit for 30 minutes.

4 Preheat the oven to 350°F. Line two sheet pans with parchment paper.

5 Scoop 24 tablespoons of the dough onto the prepared pans and spread each scoop 3–4 inches apart. Bake for 10 to 12 minutes, until lightly browned. Remove from the oven and cool on a wire rack set over a sheet of parchment paper.

6 Drizzle the cooled cookies with the melted white chocolate and let it set.

I GREW UP IN A TOWN CALLED SANDWICH

〰〰〰〰〰〰〰

I did! I grew up in Sandwich, Massachusetts. It's a small town on Cape Cod, where they grow the best cranberries in the whole world. I worked at a restaurant called Sandwich Pizza. It was a pizza place, not a sandwich shop. Well, it was a shop *in* Sandwich, so I guess it technically was a Sandwich shop. Just not a *sandwich* shop. Although we did make really good sandwiches.

It was at this restaurant that I realized I wanted to become a chef. Sandwich has the best clam chowder in the world. And the best stuffed quahogs. The best ones in Sandwich are at a place called Marshland restaurant. It's right on the salt marsh, super close to the beach. I graduated from Sandwich High School, but I didn't learn how to make sandwiches there. I took woodshop instead. My lacrosse jersey said "Sandwich" on the front and all my friends in college thought that was my nickname. There's a really cool glass factory in Sandwich and they make pink glass called cranberry glass, but I don't think they use cranberry juice. There's a place called Joe's Lobster Mart that has a stuffed 32-pound lobster on the wall.

Sandwich is really great, but if you go and make a sandwich in Sandwich, do it right. If you don't, someone will call the Sandwich Police.

GLUTEN-
FREE
COOKIES

IF YOU GOTTA SKIP THE WHEAT FLOUR, here are some good basic recipes for different kinds of gluten-free cookies that you can tweak to make your own. Some of these recipes use a flour replacer, and some are just naturally gluten-free. Gluten-free cookies are great! They offer a whole new variety of cookie textures that you just can't get when you use wheat flour.

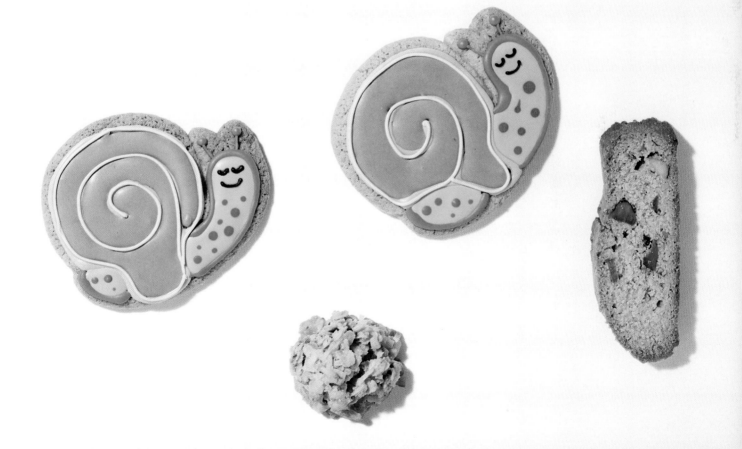

MAKES 24 COOKIES

Gluten-Free
SUGAR
• COOKIES •

Every baker needs a good sugar cookie recipe in their back pocket. You can bake this cookie super blond, or you can let it get some color on it and become crispier. This sugar cookie is great both ways. I like them a little crispier and darker because I love the flavor, but the soft version is easier to eat after it's been decorated. Sprinkles stick to soft cookies better than crispy cookies.

❶ In a large bowl, cream the butter and sugar using a stand or hand mixer. Add the egg, milk, vanilla, salt, and cinnamon. Beat to combine. Add the flour and mix to combine. If the dough is crumbly, add a splash of milk. Wrap in plastic wrap and refrigerate for 1 hour.

❷ Preheat the oven to 350°F. Line two sheet pans with parchment paper.

❸ Roll the dough out to ¼ inch thick and cut out shapes. Place the cookies on the prepared pans and freeze for 15 minutes.

❹ Bake for 10 to 12 minutes, until the cookies begin to turn golden brown. Remove from the oven and cool on a wire rack.

INGREDIENTS

½ cup (1 stick/113 grams)	**butter**, at room temperature
1 cup (200 grams)	**granulated sugar**
1	**large egg**
1 tablespoon (15 grams)	**whole milk**, plus a splash more if needed
1 teaspoon	**pure vanilla extract**
Pinch of	**kosher salt**
Pinch of	**ground cinnamon**
2 cups (240 grams)	**gluten-free all-purpose flour**

WHAT IS GLUTEN?

I bet you hear a lot about gluten, so it might be cool to know what it is, exactly. Gluten is the thing in wheat flour that makes bagels chewy and cakes tender. Gluten is a protein, and it gives anything made with wheat flour its structure. That's why cakes are light and fluffy. Wheat flour is made of starch and protein (and lots of other stuff like ash), but it is mainly those two compounds. The starch is what makes flour able to absorb moisture and get gooey enough to be mixed. When you mix a batter, the protein (aka the gluten) gets stretched out into long strands that wrap around each other and form a net. The net traps oxygen and carbon dioxide (air), and when the batter is put in the oven, the air heats up and expands. Because the gluten in the flour is stretchy, it captures the air, the air expands, and your cake rises.

Gluten-Free
CHOCOLATE CHIP
· COOKIES ·

INGREDIENTS

10 tablespoons (1¼ sticks/140 grams)	**butter**, at room temperature
1 cup (200 grams)	**granulated sugar**
1 tablespoon (20 grams)	**molasses**
1	**large egg**
2 teaspoons	**pure vanilla extract**
2¾ cups (310 grams)	**almond flour**
Pinch of	**kosher salt**
1 teaspoon	**baking soda**
12 ounces (340 grams)	**chocolate chips** (milk or dark)

I love chocolate chip cookies. One thing I love about them is that there so many different species of chocolate chip cookie. Some are thin and crispy. Some are fat and chewy. Some have all kinds of stuff in them like dried fruit or nuts. This cookie is a little crunchy on the outside and goes really well with a glass of milk.

1 Preheat the oven to 350°F. Line two sheet pans with parchment paper.

2 In a large bowl, cream the butter and sugar using a stand or hand mixer. Add the molasses, egg, and vanilla and beat for 2 minutes. Add the almond flour, salt, and baking soda and mix to combine. Fold in the chocolate chips by hand.

3 Scoop 2-ounce portions of the dough onto the prepared pans. Gently push each portion down into a thick disc shape. Bake for 18 to 20 minutes, until the cookies are golden brown and just set in the middle. Remove from the oven and cool on a wire rack.

MAKES 24 COOKIES

Gluten-Free
MOLASSES
· COOKIES ·

The holidays just ain't the holidays without molasses cookies. These are crispy on the outside and chewy in the middle but *only if you don't overbake them.* Seriously, don't overbake these cookies. When they are baked all the way through, they are fine, but when they are soft in the middle, they are fantastic.

1 In a large bowl, cream the butter, almond butter, brown sugar, and molasses using a stand or hand mixer. Scrape the bowl and add the egg, vanilla, cinnamon, ginger, and salt. Beat for 2 minutes. Add the flour and baking soda and mix to combine. Refrigerate the dough for 45 minutes.

2 Preheat the oven to 350°F. Line two sheet pans with parchment paper.

3 Put some granulated sugar in a small bowl. Scoop 24 tablespoon portions of dough, roll into smooth round balls, and then roll the balls in the sugar to coat. Place the dough balls on the prepared pans and gently press them down into thick discs. Bake for 9 to 10 minutes, until the cookies are just set. Remove from the oven and cool on a wire rack. Store at room temperature.

INGREDIENTS

4 tablespoons (½ stick/53 grams)	**butter**, at room temperature
¼ cup (62 grams)	**almond butter**
½ cup (106 grams)	lightly packed **brown sugar**
¼ cup (70 grams)	**molasses**
1	**large egg**
1 teaspoon	**pure vanilla extract**
1 teaspoon	**ground cinnamon**
1 teaspoon	**ground ginger**
Pinch of	**kosher salt**
1¼ cups (150 grams)	**gluten-free all-purpose flour**
½ teaspoon	**baking soda**
	granulated sugar, for rolling

WHAT IS MOLASSES?

Blackstrap molasses comes from sugarcane. To make sugar, sugarcane is crushed and the juice is extracted. The juice is boiled down until the water evaporates and the sugar crystallizes. The crystallized sugar gets separated from all the other stuff, which gets boiled again, producing more sugar. It's boiled one more time, and when the sugar is taken out, the other stuff has turned into a super-dark bittersweet syrup called molasses. Molasses is wonderful and delicious. When you bake with molasses, not only does it make things taste complex and rich, it also makes things chewier because molasses is wet and syrupy. Molasses is also good for you! It has lots of vitamins and minerals like potassium, vitamin B, and zinc.

MAKES 36 COOKIES

Gluten-Free

COCONUT OATMEAL

· COOKIES ·

These are some of the easiest cookies in this book to make. I like chunks in my oatmeal cookies. I like stuff. Oatmeal cookies need lots of junk in them—nuts, dried fruits, chocolate chips, all kinds of stuff. Coconut works perfectly because it's delicious, and it adds that super unique coconut texture to the cookies.

1 Preheat the oven to 325°F. Line two sheet pans with parchment paper.

2 In a large bowl, beat the coconut oil, brown sugar, and salt for 2 minutes. Add the egg and vanilla and beat until smooth. Stir in the oats and coconut flakes by hand. Refrigerate for 15 minutes.

3 Scoop 36 tablespoon portions of the dough onto the prepared pans. Bake for 10 to 12 minutes, or until the cookies start to turn golden brown. Remove from the oven and cool on a wire rack.

INGREDIENTS

½ cup (109 grams)	**coconut oil**
½ cup (106 grams)	lightly packed **brown sugar**
Pinch of	**kosher salt**
1	**large egg**
1 teaspoon	**pure vanilla extract**
2 cups (160 grams)	**gluten-free rolled oats**
1½ cups (145 grams)	**sweetened coconut flakes**

MAKES 18 COOKIES

Gluten-Free Almond Flour
BISCOTTI

This is a delicious cookie that is naturally gluten-free, and the almond flavor works perfectly for biscotti. These have a delicious cardamom glaze, but they also go great with chocolate.

MAKE THE COOKIES

1 Preheat the oven to 350°F. Line a sheet pan with parchment paper.

2 In a large bowl, beat the brown sugar, eggs, coconut oil, almond extract, vanilla, and salt. Add the almond flour, pistachios, and baking powder. Beat until a dough forms.

3 Roll the dough into a log about 3 inches wide and place it on the prepared pan. Bake for 20 to 22 minutes, until the log is golden brown. Remove from the oven and cool on a wire rack for 20 to 25 minutes. Lower the oven temperature to 300°F.

4 Slice the log into ¾-inch-thick segments. Lay them flat on the pan and bake for 10 minutes, then flip and bake for another 10 minutes. Remove from the oven and cool completely on a wire rack set over a sheet of parchment paper.

OPTIONAL: GLAZE

5 In a small bowl, whisk together the powdered sugar, milk, cardamom, and salt. Adjust the consistency with more milk or powdered sugar. Drizzle the glaze over one side of the biscotti and let it set.

INGREDIENTS

FOR THE COOKIES

½ cup (106 grams)	lightly packed **brown sugar**
2	**large eggs**
2 tablespoons (27 grams)	**coconut oil**
½ teaspoon	**almond extract**
½ teaspoon	**pure vanilla extract**
Pinch of	**kosher salt**
2 cups (224 grams)	**almond flour**
½ cup (65 grams)	**shelled pistachios**, lightly toasted and roughly chopped or smashed
1 teaspoon	**baking powder**

FOR THE GLAZE **(OPTIONAL)**

1 cup (130 grams)	**powdered sugar**, plus more if needed
2 tablespoons (30 grams)	**whole milk**, plus more if needed
1 teaspoon	**ground cardamom**
Pinch of	**kosher salt**

MACARONS

YOU'VE PROBABLY HAD A MACARON. And I bet you loved it. Macarons have the most intricate of textures in such a cute, tiny cookie. The outside is a super-thin layer of crunch. The inside is soft and chewy. In between is usually something gooey, like caramel, buttercream, or jam. All together, those things create an absolutely magical little bite. They can be tricky to get just right, so be patient. I promise that even when you don't get perfect macarons they'll still be delicious.

Basic
MACARONS

INGREDIENTS

FOR THE COOKIES

1 cup (130 grams)	**powdered sugar**
½ cup (140 grams)	**almond flour**
3 (100 grams)	**egg whites**
Pinch of	**cream of tartar**
½ cup (90 grams)	**granulated sugar**
1 teaspoon	**pure vanilla extract**
Pinch of	**kosher salt**
	food coloring

FOR THE BUTTERCREAM

1 cup (2 sticks/225 grams)	**butter**, at room temperature
1 teaspoon	**pure vanilla extract**
Pinch of	**kosher salt**
3 cups (600 grams)	**granulated sugar**
¼ cup (60 grams)	**whole milk**
	food coloring

This is my basic macaron recipe. Get it down and then start messing around with different flavors and nut flours. It's very customizable. There are a lot of details in the method on how to make these things. Macarons can be really tricky until you get the hang of it, but once you do, you'll feel like a real-life pastry chef! I know I do. Pro tip: These cookies make *the best* gifts. Get a cute box and make someone's day.

MAKE THE COOKIES

❶ Line two sheet pans with parchment paper. Using a 1½-inch round cutter, trace circles onto the parchment, making sure to draw them dark enough that you can see them from the opposite side of the parchment. Flip the parchment so the circles are facing the pan. This will be your guide when piping the macarons. Fit a piping bag with a large plain tip.

❷ Put the powdered sugar and almond flour in the bowl of a food processor and buzz for 2 to 3 minutes. Pour the mixture into a fine-mesh strainer and sift it into a big bowl. If there are any big pieces left over in the strainer, toss them. This will ensure that the tops of the cookies are smooth.

3 Put the egg whites in the bowl of a stand mixer fitted with the whisk attachment and start whisking on medium speed. Add the cream of tartar, then, when the eggs start getting foamy, slowly stream in the granulated sugar. Continue whipping until stiff peaks form. Add the vanilla, salt, and food coloring at this point.

4 Add one-third of the almond mixture to the egg whites and gently fold with a rubber spatula. Add the rest of the almond mixture and gently fold until the batter looks like thick lava. Transfer the batter to the piping bag. Glue the parchment down to the sheet pans by putting a dot of batter in each corner of the pan and pressing the parchment against it. Pipe the batter onto the parchment, using the circles you drew as your guide. Bang the sheet pans on the counter a few times to help the macarons settle. Pop any air bubbles that you see. Put the sheet pans out of the way and let the macarons air-dry for 45 minutes to 1 hour. When they're ready to bake, you should be able to gently touch them without the batter sticking to your finger.

5 Preheat the oven to 300°F.

MAKE THE BUTTERCREAM

6 In a large bowl, cream the butter, vanilla, and salt. Add the granulated sugar one spoonful at a time. Drizzle in the milk until you like the consistency. You probably won't need all of it. Drink the extra. It's good for you. Now mix in the food coloring to get your desired color. Let sit at room temperature until the macaron shells have finished baking.

7 Bake the cookies for 7 minutes, then rotate the pans and bake for about 7 more minutes. The macarons shouldn't brown at all. Remove from the oven and cool on the pans.

8 To assemble the macarons, pipe some of the buttercream onto the flat side of a macaron, then sandwich with the flat side of another one. Store in an airtight container in the fridge.

Macaron Fillings

You can put *anything* in a macaron, and it'll be delicious. Ganache? Yup.
Jam? Absolutely. Buttercream? Totally. Pulled pork? Uh . . . Buttercream is a very
traditional filling for macarons because it's so versatile. You can add spices,
jam, extracts, or nuts, infuse it with tea, color it—you name it, you can do it. It even goes
well with other kinds of fillings: chocolate, jams and jellies, even peanut butter!
So it's good to start to know how to make buttercream.

E-Z American Buttercream

Makes enough for 25–30 macarons

1 cup (2 sticks/226 grams)	**butter**
Pinch of	**kosher salt**
3½ cups (450 grams)	**powdered sugar**
4 tablespoons (60 grams)	**whole milk**

In the bowl of a stand mixer fitted with the paddle attachment or in a large bowl using a hand mixer, beat the butter and salt until light and smooth. Give the bowl a good scrape, add the powdered sugar, and beat until fluffy. Drizzle in the milk if you want the buttercream a little thinner. At this point, add any flavoring and color you want. Vanilla, cinnamon, blue, raspberry jam—totally your call.

Whipped Ganache

Makes enough for 25–30 macarons

FOR DARK CHOCOLATE GANACHE

4 ounces (113 grams)	**dark chocolate,** chopped
Pinch of	**kosher salt**
Splash of	**pure vanilla extract**
½ cup (113 grams)	**heavy cream**

FOR WHITE CHOCOLATE GANACHE

1¼ cups (212 grams)	**white chocolate chips**
2 tablespoons (25 grams)	**butter**
Pinch of	**kosher salt**
⅔ cup (160 grams)	**heavy cream**

Put all the ingredients except the cream in a bowl. Pour the cream into a small saucepan and heat over medium-high heat until it comes to a boil. Immediately pour the hot cream into the bowl over the chocolate. Cover with a clean kitchen towel and wait 5 minutes. With a whisk, gently stir until the chocolate melts completely and the mixture comes together. Let cool to room temperature and then whip with a whisk until fluffy. Store at room temperature.

Mango Ganache

Makes enough for 25–30 macarons

1	ripe **mango**, peeled, pitted, and chopped
1 cup (150 grams)	chopped **white chocolate**
Pinch of	**kosher salt**

❶ Puree the mango in the bowl of a food processor until smooth. Strain the puree through a fine-mesh strainer and set aside.

❷ Melt the white chocolate with the salt using a double boiler. Remove from the heat and stir in the mango puree. Let it cool in the fridge.

PRO TIP: You can try this recipe with any pureed fruit. Just make sure you have about ½ cup (120 grams) of puree after you strain it. If you have extra puree, make a smoothie.

Pistachio Filling

Makes enough for 25–30 macarons

¼ cup (30 grams)	**shelled pistachios**
¼ cup (60 grams)	**cream cheese**, at room temperature
2 tablespoons (25 grams)	**butter**, at room temperature
1 cup (120 grams)	**powdered sugar**
Pinch of	**kosher salt**

❶ Pulse the pistachios in a blender until you get a relatively fine meal.

❷ In the bowl of a stand mixer fitted with the paddle attachment or in a large bowl using a hand mixer, beat the cream cheese, butter, and salt together. Scrape the bowl and add the pistachio flour. Beat for 2 minutes. Add the powdered sugar. Beat until smooth, scraping the bowl a few times to make sure everything is mixed in. Store at room temperature.

PRO TIP: This recipe works with any nut. Also, you might have to put more than ¼ cup (30 grams) of pistachios in the blender to get it to work. Sometimes really small amounts are too small.

Fancy Macarons

Round macarons are super cute and delicious, but there is a whole wide world of different things you can make with macarons. Here are a few ideas to get your creative juices flowing. For decorations, I like to use marzipan, not fondant. Marzipan tastes much better and goes with the almond flour in the recipe.

Cactus macaron

1 Color your macaron batter three different shades of green. Bake them in circles—small, medium, and large.

2 Mash up a soft-baked brownie, shape it into a mound, and cover with graham cracker crumbs.

3 Fill the macarons. Put a toothpick into the brownie mound. Place the largest circle on its side and stick it on the toothpick. Stick smaller macarons on their sides on top of the large circle to create cactus leaves.

4 Decorate with royal icing cactus spines and a little red marzipan flower.

Teddy bear macaron

1 Color your macaron batter whatever color you want for the bears.

2 Pipe a circle, then pipe two smaller circles that just touch the larger circle where the ears should go. Bake the macarons.

3 Fill the macarons with ganache, then make the nose and the inside of the ears with colored marzipan. Use royal icing for the eyes and any other facial features.

Hamburger macaron

1 Color your macaron batter a hamburger bun color. Bake them in circles with sesame seeds on top.

2 Make lettuce, tomatoes, onions, and cheese with colored marzipan.

3 Use chocolate ganache for the burger.

4 Assemble the burgers.

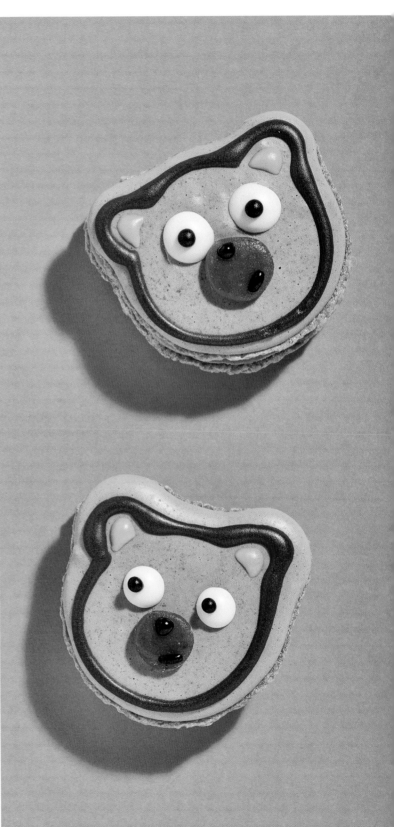

GLOSSARY

Batch: an amount of baked goods made at one time

Batter: a semi-liquid combination of ingredients that is looser than dough

Beat: to mix ingredients together quickly, often with a whisk or mixer, which smooths and adds air into the mixture

Blend: to mix together two ingredients until they don't separate

Boil: to heat a liquid to its boiling point, above 212°F, or adding an ingredient into a boiling liquid

Buttercream: a fluffy frosting used to coat or decorate baked goods, which is made by creaming butter with powdered sugar and other ingredients

Caramelize: to heat sugar until it turns a golden brown

Chill: to cool food to less than room temperature

Chop: to cut food into small pieces

Coat: to coat a food with another ingredient

Combine: to mix two or more ingredients

Consistency: a food's texture, such as thin or thick

Cool: to allow a warm food to reduce in temperature

Cream: to mix ingredients into softened butter

Crust: the hard outer shell of a bread or pie

Dissolve: to incorporate a solid ingredient into a liquid

Double boil: to gradually melt an ingredient such as butter or chocolate over a pot of simmering water

Drizzle: to pour a thin stream of liquid over a food

Dust: to sprinkle a thin layer of an ingredient over a food

Egg wash: a beaten egg mixture or brushing a beaten egg mixture over a food

Fold: to gently incorporate, often with a spatula, a light ingredient into a heavier ingredient

Garnish: to decorate a food

Gluten: proteins in grains that give food shape

Grain: plant seeds from crops such as wheat

Grainy: describing the sandy texture of a food

Grease: to coat a pan with oil, cooking spray, or butter to stop food from sticking

Melt: to heat a solid ingredient until it is a liquid

Mix: to combine two or more ingredients until blended

Pinch: an amount of a dry ingredient, such as salt, that can be held between the thumb and forefinger

Pipe: to squeeze a liquid through a piping bag for decorating

Preheat: to heat an oven or pan to a specific temperature before putting food inside

Pulse: to repeatedly turn on and off a blender/mixer to mix ingredients quickly but not fully

Scrape: to use a flat or sharp tool to remove something from a surface

Simmer: to heat a liquid to just below the boiling point

Soft peaks: to whip egg whites or cream until they slump over when you pull a spoon out

Soften: to leave butter or margarine at room temperature until it can be easily spread

Sprinkle: to lightly scatter an ingredient over a food

Stiff peaks: to whip egg whites or cream until they stand up straight when you pull a spoon out

Stir: to use a slow circular motion either to combine ingredients or to stop food from burning

Whip: to stir a food using a fork, whisk, or mixer with short, quick movements

Whisk: to use a kitchen tool to beat and add air to a mixture

MEASUREMENT CONVERSIONS

Equivalent Measurements

1 tablespoon = 3 teaspoons = .5 ounce = 15 milliliter

¼ cup = 4 tablespoons = 2 ounces = 59 milliliters

⅓ cup = 5 tablespoons = 3 ounces = 79 milliliters

½ cup = 8 tablespoons = 4 ounces = 118 milliliters

⅔ cup = 11 tablespoons = 5 ounces = 158 milliliters

1 cup = 16 tablespoons = 8 ounces = 237 milliliters

1 gallon = 4 quarts = 8 pints = 16 cups = 3.8 liters

1 quart = 2 pints = 4 cups = 950 milliliters

1 pint = 2 cups = 500 milliliters

1 pound = 16 ounces

½ pound = 8 ounces

BUTTER

½ stick = 4 tablespoons = ¼ cup

1 stick = 8 tablespoons = ½ cup

Equivalent Temperatures

275° F	140° C	Very Cool
300° F	150° C	Cool
325° F	165° C	Warm
350° F	177° C	Moderate
375° F	190° C	Moderate
400° F	200° C	Moderately Hot
425° F	220° C	Hot
450° F	230° C	Hot
475° F	245° C	Hot
500° F	260° C	Very Hot

INDEX

NOTE: Page numbers in *italic* refer to photos.

A

Alfajores, *76, 77*
Almond Cookies
    Blorbs, Oatmeal Coconut Chocolate, 48, *49*
    Chinese, *68,* 69
Almond Flour Biscotti, Gluten-Free, 194, *195*
Animal Crackers, 110, *111*

B

Basic Macarons, 198–199, *199*
Biscotti, 78, *79*
    Gluten-Free Almond Flour, 194, *195*
Black and White Cookies, 152–153, *153*
Brownies, Cookie, 138, *139*
Brown sugar, white sugar vs., 159
Butter, Cookie, *150,* 151
Buttercream, E-Z American, 201
Butterscotch Milk Chocolate Cookies, *46, 47*

C

Cactus Macaron, 202
Candy Cane Sugar Cookies, 168, *169*
Cape Cod Cranberry Cookies, 182, *183*
Cardamom Pistachio Laddu, *72, 73*
Checkerboard Cookies, Rainbow, *108,* 109
Chinese Almond Cookies, *68,* 69
Chocolate
    Blorbs, Oatmeal Coconut Almond, 48, *49*
    Crinkle Cookies, 164, *165*
    Double, Drop Cookies, 62, *63*
    Filling, 173
    Milk, Butterscotch Cookies, *46, 47*
    Peanut Butter No-Bake Cookies, 44, *45*
    White, Gingersnaps, *42,* 43
Chocolate Chip Cookies, Gluten-Free, *188,* 189
Coconut
    Blorbs, Oatmeal Almond Chocolate, 48, *49*
    Macaroons, *56,* 57
    Oatmeal Cookies, Gluten-Free, *192,* 193

Cookie Brownies, 138, *139*
Cookie Butter, *150,* 151
Cookie Cake, Giant, 132, *133*
Cookie-crumb crusts, 134–135, *135*
Cookie Dough, Edible, 148, *149*
Cookie philosophy, *8,* 9
Cookie Pie, Peanut Butter, *140,* 141
Cookies
    as an ingredient (*See* Things with cookies in them)
    decorating, *174,* 174–175
    drop, 58
    history of, 102–103, *103*
    preparing to bake, *24, 25*
    things that are sort of like (*See* Sorta cookies)
Cookie Salad, 142–143, *143*
Cookies 'n' Cream Ice Cream, No-Churn, *144,* 145
Cranberry Cookies, Cape Cod, 182, *183*
Crinkle Cookies, Chocolate, 164, *165*

D

Date
    Cookies, Ramadan, *176,* 177
    Rugelach, Walnut &, *170,* 171
Decorated cookies, *122,* 122–133, *123*
    Giant Cookie Cake, 132, *133*
    Royal Icing (with Egg Whites), 127
    Royal Icing (with Meringue Powder), 127
    royal icing for, *126,* 126–131, *128–131* (*See also* Royal icing)
    Sugar Cookies, 124, *125*
Decorating cookies, *174,* 174–175
Double Chocolate Drop Cookies, 62, *63*
Drop Cookies, 58
    Double Chocolate, 62, *63*
Duff's Killer Pecan Cookies, *34,* 35

E

Edible Cookie Dough, 148, *149*
Equipment, 14–15, *15–19*
E-Z American Buttercream, 201

F

Fancy Macarons, 202, *202, 203*
Favorite cookies, 50–51, *51*
Filling
    Chocolate, 173
    Pistachio, 201
    Prune, 173
Flooding royal icing, 127, *130*
    directions for, 131
    recipes for, 127
Florentines, *90,* 91
Fortune Cookies, 114, *115*
    history of, 114

G

Ganache
    Mango, 201
    Whipped, 201
Giant Cookie Cake, 132, *133*
Gingerbread Pine Cones, *166,* 167
Gingersnaps, White Chocolate, *42,* 43
Glossary, 204
Gluten, 186
Gluten-Free cookies, *184,* 184–195, *185*
    Almond Flour Biscotti, 194, *195*
    Chocolate Chip Cookies, *188,* 189
    Coconut Oatmeal Cookies, *192,* 193
    Molasses Cookies, 190, *191*
    Sugar Cookies, 186, *187*

H

Hamantaschen, 172–173, *173*
    Chocolate Filling, 173
    Prune Filling, 173
Hamburger Macaron, 202, *202, 203*
Haystack Cookies, 58, *59*
History
    of cookies, 102–103, *103*
    of fortune cookies, 114
Holiday cookies, *162,* 162–183, *163*
    Candy Cane Sugar Cookies, 168, *169*
    Cape Cod Cranberry Cookies, 182, *183*
    Chocolate Crinkle Cookies, 164, *165*
    Date & Walnut Rugelach, *170,* 171
    decorating, *174,* 174–175
    Gingerbread Pine Cones, *166,* 167
    Hamantaschen, 172–173, *173*
    Pecan Tassies, *180,* 181
    PSL Cookies, 178, *179*
    Ramadan Date Cookies, *176,* 177

I

Ice Cream
    Cookies 'n' Cream, No-Churn, *144,* 145
    Sandwiches, No-Churn Classic, 100–101, *101*
Ice Cream Cones, 156, *157*
Ingredients, 20–22, *21–23*
    cookies as (*See* Things with cookies in them)
International cookies, *64–67,* 64–87
    Alfajores, *76,* 77
    Biscotti, 78, *79*
    Cardamom Pistachio Laddu, *72,* 73
    Chinese Almond Cookies, *68,* 69
    Kanom Ping, 74, *75*
    Mooncakes, 70–71, *71*
    Pfeffernuesse, 82, *83*
    Scottish Shortbread, 86, *87*
    Tahini Cookies, 80, *81*
    Tortas de Aceite, *84,* 85

K

Kanom Ping, 74, *75*
Kitchen basics, 12–13, *13*
Kitchen safety, 10–11, *11*

L

Lace Cookies, *30*, 31
Laddu, Cardamom Pistachio, *72,* 73
Linzer Cookies, *98,* 99

M

Macaron(s), *196*, 196–203, *197*
    Basic, 198–199, *200*
    Cactus, 202
    E-Z American Buttercream, 201
    Fancy, 202, *202, 203*
    fillings for, *200,* 200–201
    Hamburger, 202, *202, 203*
    Mango Ganache, 201
    Pistachio Filling, 201
    Teddy Bear, 202, *203*
    Whipped Ganache, 201
Macaroons, 57
    Coconut, *56,* 57
Mandelbrot, 118, *119*
Mango Ganache, 201
Measurement conversions, 205
Meringue Cookies, Rainbow, 113, *114*
Milk Chocolate Butterscotch Cookies, *46,* 47
Milk-&-cookie moments, 120, *121*
Molasses, 190
    Cookies, Gluten-Free, 190, *191*
Mooncakes, 70–71, *71*
Moravian Spice Cookies, 32, *33*
Mound cookies, *52,* 52–63, *53*
    Coconut Macaroons, *56,* 57
    Double Chocolate Drop Cookies, 62, *63*
    Haystack Cookies, 58, *59*
    Oatmeal Nugs, 61, *61*
    Polvorones, 54–55, *55*

N

N'awlins Pralines, *154,* 155
New Orleans, 155
No-Bake Cookies, Chocolate Peanut Butter, 44, *45*
No-Churn Classic Ice Cream Sandwiches, 100–101, *101*
No-Churn Cookies 'n' Cream Ice Cream, *144,* 145

O

Oatmeal
    Blorbs, Coconut Almond Chocolate, 48, *49*
    Coconut Cookies, Gluten-Free, *192,* 193
    Nugs, 61, *61*
Oh-Wee-Ohs, *94,* 95

P

Painting on royal icing, 131, *131*
Peanut Butter
    Chocolate No-Bake Cookies, 44, *45*
    Cookie Pie, *140,* 141
Pecan
    Cookies, Duff's Killer, *34,* 35
    Tassies, *180,* 181
Pfeffernuesse, 82, *83*
Piping royal icing, *126,* 127, *129*
    directions for, 129
    recipes for, 127
Pistachio
    Cardamom Laddu, *72,* 73
    Filling, 201
Polvorones, 54–55, *55*
Pralines, N'awlins, *154,* 155
Preparing to bake, 24, 25, *25*
Prune Filling, 173
PSL Cookies, 178, *179*

R

Rainbow Checkerboard Cookies, *108,* 109
Rainbow Meringue Cookies, 113, *114*
Ramadan Date Cookies, *176,* 177
Recipes, writing, 36, *37*
Rolled Wafer Cookies, *116,* 117
Royal Icing, 126–131
    directions for, 128, *128*
    flooding, 127, *130,* 131
    painting on, 131, *131*
    piping, *126,* 127, 129, *129*
    recipes for, 127
Royal Icing (with Egg Whites), 127
    for flooding, 127
    for piping, 127
Royal Icing (with Meringue Powder), 127
    for flooding, 127
    for piping, 127
Rugelach, Date & Walnut, *170,* 171

S

Safety, 10–11, *11*
Salad, Cookie, 142–143, *143*
Sandwich, Massachusetts, 183
Sandwich cookies, *88,* 88–101, *89*
    Florentines, *90,* 91
    Linzer Cookies, *98,* 99
    No-Churn Classic Ice Cream Sandwiches, 100–101, *101*
    Oh-Wee-Ohs, *94,* 95
    S'more Cookies, 96, *97*
    Stroopwafels, 92–93, *93*
Scottish Shortbread, 86, *87*
S'more Cookies, 96, *97*
Sorta cookies, *146,* 146–158, *147*
    Black and White Cookies, 152–153, *153*
    Cookie Butter, *150,* 151

Edible Cookie Dough, 148, *149*
    Graham Crackers, 158, *160–161*
    Ice Cream Cones, 156, *157*
    N'awlins Pralines, *154,* 155
Spice Cookies, Moravian, 32, *33*
Spritz Cookies, 106, *107*
Stroopwafels, 92–93, *93*
Sugar, brown vs. white, 159
Sugar Cookies, 124, *125*
    Candy Cane, 168, *169*
    Gluten-Free, 186, *187*

T

Tahini Cookies, *80,* 81
Teddy Bear Macaron, 202, *203*
Thick cookies, *38,* 38–49, *39*
    Chocolate Peanut Butter No-Bake Cookies, 44, *45*
    Milk Chocolate Butterscotch Cookies, 46, *47*
    Oatmeal Coconut Almond Chocolate Blorbs, 48, *49*
    Thumbprint Cookies, 40, *41*
    White Chocolate Gingersnaps, *42,* 43
Thin cookies, *26,* 26–35, *27*
    Duff's Killer Pecan Cookies, *34,* 35
    Lace Cookies, *30,* 31
    Moravian Spice Cookies, 32, *33*
    Tuiles, 28, *29*
Things with cookies in them, *136,* 136–145, *137*
    Cookie Brownies, 138, *139*
    Cookie Salad, 142–143, *143*
    No-Churn Cookies 'n' Cream Ice Cream, *144,* 145
    Peanut Butter Cookie Pie, *140,* 141
Thumbprint Cookies, 40, *41*
Tortas de Aceite, *84,* 85
Tuiles, 28, *29*

U

Unclassifiable cookies, *104,* 104–119, *105*
    Animal Crackers, 110, *111*
    Fortune Cookies, 114, *115*
    Mandelbrot, 118, *119*
    Rainbow Checkerboard Cookies, *108,* 109
    Rainbow Meringue Cookies, 113, *114*
    Rolled Wafer Cookies, *116,* 117
    Spritz Cookies, 106, *107*

W

Wafer Cookies, Rolled, *116,* 117
Whipped Ganache, 201
White Chocolate Gingersnaps, *42,* 43
White sugar, brown sugar vs., 159
Writing recipes, 36, *37*

ACKNOWLEDGMENTS

Books are a LOT of work! It takes a whole group of friends to make a book. My friends Ali Tila and Lauren Feldman baked ALL the cookies with me and helped me figure out what to do when something would go wrong. They also made the cookies look really good so my friends Benjamin Turner and Mai could set them up in cool poses and take really awesome pictures of them. My friends from down the street, Tracey and Andrew Rosen, helped us out with some macaron malfunctions. My good friend Molly Yeh taught me about cookie salad and helped me create one of my very own. My friend Shirley Chung taught us all how to make mooncakes and brought us delicious dumplings that we ate like troglodytes. My new friend Noah Leopold got us stuff when we ran out and made sure we had everything we needed to make all these cookies. My friends Andy Stabile, Andrianna Yeatts, and Kari Stuart were the adults who did all the business stuff that I'm not good at. My friends David Linker, Rick Farley, and Ellen Scordato made sure the book looks as good as the cookies and that I spelled everything correctly. My friend Lisa Shotland made sure everyone did their jobs, and made sure the cookies were where they were supposed to be, and made sure that basically everything was done. She probably had the hardest job because sometimes I forget stuff. My best friend in the whole world (and my wife), Johnna, and my daughter, Josephine, made sure each and every cookie tasted good. Seriously, everyone. Thanks.